AF448914

The Spy, A.D. 2150-2154

By: Tom Ball

Copyright© 2023 Tom Ball
ISBN: 978-93-95224-57-4

First Edition: 2023
Rs. 200/-

Cyberwit.net
HIG 45 Kaushambi Kunj, Kalindipuram
Allahabad - 211011 (U.P.) India
http://www.cyberwit.net
Tel: +(91) 9415091004
E-mail: info@cyberwit.net

No part of this book may be reproduced or transmitted in any form or by
any means, electronic, mechanical, photocopying, or otherwise, without
the express written consent of Tom Ball.

Printed at VCORE.

Contents

PART ONE: 2150: SPRING/SUMMER

I, Mary Q., served the US Secret Service faithfully. I was high-ranking #2, in the "Heads Department" which meant I used active and passive Mind Reading Technology (MRT) to get in the heads of radical thinkers and other dangerous and powerful people. Famous people too, as they had a lot of power. Most were mind read passively and didn't know they were being watched.

Basically, I got in heads and prevented radicals from entering politics, science or the arts. And such people were sent to rehab which cleansed their thoughts and operated on their brain and made them no longer radicals.

Some of the radicals were largely benevolent and I even loved a few of them and tried to make them more mainstream. But many were set in their ways. So, we spies debated getting in the heads of people as young as 2 (Everyone was born as an adult with memories of both parents) and decided whether to hit them. To try and nip them in the bud.

We utilized hypnosis to try and change those set in errant ways to great effect. Few people knew the power of post-hypnotic suggestion. It essentially allowed us to reprogram people and we made them forget that we had hypnotized them. But usually this was not enough, and they had to go to rehab.

I appeared to my mind reading case subjects as an ordinary, yet clever-looking persona and I kept changing faces… I was originally a Chinese American, but now typically appeared with blue skin. Changing skin color was OK with us spies as it eliminated racism.

One of my more dangerous subjects was a radical woman, Julia E., who wrote a book about a World in which radical thinkers were cloned and took over the North American Federation government. And the book featured people who were forced people to read and follow the "Thinker's Bible," which encouraged people to follow radical leaders/ writers of the past and present. The radicals she described were pro-Space and in favor of AI. But we spies had convinced governments everywhere to ban all AI, saying it was too dangerous, 30 years previously. And as time went by the power of the UW (United Worlds) was increasing dramatically and now the UW sent in troops if any one State rebelled. And in time the national governments lost most of their power to the UW. It was mostly just the Mayors and the UW. But some nations still had power. And we were closing down deep Space colonies. It was simply too dangerous to have humans years away. And as for the Thinker's Bible, it was banned and forbidden, and Julia E. was interviewed by me. I mind read, "Radicals just rock the boat and are selfish and egotistical and power-crazed. And we are approaching Utopia. No need for further Dystopian essays and novels. All art needs to be mainstream and wholesome. As for science we have achieved all we could with cures for all diseases and eternal youth and so on. So, no more new science. And you are a dangerous radical. You need to retract your Thinker's Bible, and then go to rehab." and she went quietly.

And another radical, Davida, advocated people living in spacious air cars and returning most of the land to nature. Houses and skyscrapers were to be demolished. She said that people would dock their air cars at various hubs and party on. And humans by nature were wanderers for almost all of our history. I mind read to her, "This would cause an upheaval, that is not necessary. Real estate drives much of the economy, billions of people would lose their land and homes with such a scenario. It's simply not practical. Try to think of mainstream thoughts and go easy on the radical views." And I hypnotized her to do so.

Another radical, Bob B.; I got in his head and told him to desist from advocating true love. Of course, all sex diseases had been cured. But true love would only lead to breaking bonds with the State. And would lead to rebellion and insurrection we spies figured. We wanted loyalty to the State above all. We were all in this World together, we were all in the same boat. But Bob said true love would lead to an explosion of Bohemian art. Anyway, we let him have numerous lovers, but he had to agree to no longer advocate true love publicly, and was hypnotized accordingly.

Then there was the radical Diana H., who was Vice President of North China who said, "Chinese people were superior, and it was manifest destiny that China should take over the entire Earth." Even though she was a Chinese national, she was part of the UW and we got in her head in English and hypnotized her and got her to resign from her post and pick up painting pictures instead.

Then there was the guerilla movement in Cambodia to overthrow the democratically elected government and make their leader, Ben 74, tyrant. Ben wanted to change peoples' heads with brain apps and recreate the elite minds that had been killed off during the episodes of the killing fields in the 1970s. But brain apps mostly drove people insane and there were few success stories. So, we interfered and got Ben 74 to step down and dissolve the movement., and we did hypnosis on him. Some tried to carry on without him, but it was futile.

Another radical, Meera B., President of South India, was in favor of banning MRT, saying it was too powerful and could fall into the wrong hands. But we spies controlled all the MRT in the Worlds and beyond and didn't let dictators use MRT to supress their populations. And we got in Meera's head and had her resign from politics and go to rehab.

Then there was the man who claimed to be the reincarnation of Jesus. He said, "God wanted to have the people live in peace and love." But we spies had been backing a lot of wars with rogue states; mostly we got in the leaders' heads and that was the end of the wars. But some tyrants were wary of MRT and kept everyone at a distance.

The tyrants all belonged to the UW alliance, and few dared to rebel against the UW. But we had MRT that worked with an invisible receptor within 20 yards with an ultimate unlimited range and some tyrants knew that. Anyway, we told this Jesus peace is for spies to achieve and got him to back down and we told him in his head that we were the Gods now and Jesus just didn't cut it these days.

He had told the people, there has to be a God, and everyone had a soul. This coincided with research creating a human soul out of holograms. And this Jesus condemned those who were spies and surrounded himself with followers who passed a lie detector test. But we used hypnotism to allow our agents to pass the test and so we got in his head. The range of the MRT technology was 100 m, we told our spies. But actually, we could zoom in on someone's voice from a distance of thousands of km with the right receptor link, but I thought it best if the bulk of our spies didn't realize that. Anyway I mind read with this Jesus, and he mind read, "I believe in peace and love and kindness, don't you?" I mind read, "But one has to be practical. Most people are not really kind. And if we let them, they'd probably exclusively love, love dolls. And there are some tyrants who want war, not peace. Your sizable following is of no consequence." He mind read, "One day I will have billions of followers and we will vote in our members in the World's democracies and take power everywhere." I mind read, "No you are not going to get a chance to raise hell. You need to tell your followers to back down and say that it is not the time for love. If you don't, I will drive you completely mad and your followers will totally lose respect for you." So, he tried to summon his assistants, but we yelled so loud in his head, he couldn't function, but still he tried to thwart us. His assistants suspected it was us, but they feared winding up like him, catatonic, so gradually they let the movement fade away and Jesus was sent to rehab, never to be seen again. It was kind of tragic to bring about his demise, but he simply hadn't been practical and had been power crazed.

And another one was the phenomenon of the famous rock band, "the Heat from Hell." They had millions of followers who thought of them as Gods, and they were far too powerful. So, we got in the head of the main 2 songwriters and told them no more new music. They would still be adored only people would say they had sold out to debauchery and neo heroin. And we hypnotized them.

And there was another rock band, "Kings of Vacuity." They advocated illegal drugs, like neo-heroin and "crazy drugs" and "drugs of boldness," and so we had to do something about them. So, we got them to quit cold turkey and forbid them to talk about drugs. They tried to fight us but didn't have a chance. We just kept turning up the volume until they backed down, and we hypnotized them.

Another Radical was Duane T. He was an advocate of neo-fascism and got elected in England. We the UW spies got into his head and those of his leading supporters. He was wary of MRT, but we finally got to him and he resigned. Some people remarked that no one today had any guts and kept resigning/backing down. But most were oblivious to what was truly was going on.

And then there were the Masons. They Masons, as always were powerful business entities. So, we got in their heads and broke up the organization which we saw as rivals for power. This pissed off many of the rich elite, but we told them they were too powerful as a group.

And we broke up Mensa; they too were becoming too powerful. But I fell in love with one of their brightest, Rory. He mind read, "With the right tutors, we could turn everyone into a genius." I loved him and mind read, "It is bad to have an aggressive elite, we need everyone to keep to themselves." He mind read, "But Mensa is the brain trust of the whole World." I replied, "No point in putting all our eggs in one basket. Let the geniuses be free, if they are good and not radicals." He said, "But you spies think all thinkers are radicals." I told him, "I, for example am very clever but I follow the rules of the US Secret Service and thereby serve the public. I am an insider, not an outsider." Anyway, I loved him for weeks and let my work lapse a bit. I didn't know why I loved him so much. It was the closest I'd come so far to true love. So I knew it was wrong and broke up with him before I lost control of myself.

Then next up I was hot on the trail of a radical, Timothy T., who owned a news broadcasting service Online. He wanted to beam his service even to Space, where there were a number of colonies and he wanted exclusive rights to Space broadcasting believing it to be the future which really mattered. He was radical in that all his news was highbrow and thought everyone in Space should be a genius of one kind or another. I told him in his head that, "You seemed to be trying to make Space for the clever only and this was an anathema; Space should be for everyone." But he mind read, "The future belongs to the clever and soon Superhumans would be taking over. And clever AI would reign supreme." I mind read, "AI is not human; we will lose control over humanity with these machines." He mind read, "Humanity is the creator of these machines!" Anyway, we forced him to step down as head of the company and we set up Space lotteries in which ordinary people could come to Space. And I was very pleased. After that some spies said we were like a communist regime, forcing everyone to be equal. But we felt that all human life was precious. Or at least that's what we told one another, but some of us were in favor of the radical Timothy T, who they said had his heart in the right place. But most of us felt he was too powerful. He said, "Mind reading was the great equalizer, and leveled the playing field." And some wanted him to be a spy… So, we hypnotized him to spy and find radicals.

And us spies forced the breakup of many mega-companies as the CEOs were too powerful. One of them was a CEO of the biggest bank who had gotten rich from Space real estate speculation and the bank controlled many colonies in Space. The bank's headquarters was in "Sin City," Mars. And I was one of the spies to get into his head. I mind read with him, "You are too powerful!" He mind read, "I was helping to broaden the human experience and science was developing faster speeds to enhance the experience. And terraforming technology and new hardy plants were leading to new science for the benefit of humankind. And he wanted supercomputers to produce numerous androids and holograms." I mind read to him, "Surely androids and holograms are not the future!" He mind read, "But they can survive anywhere and Space is so vast." I asked him mind reading, "Why the rush to Space and trying to replace humans?" And I mind read, "Do you hate humans?" He mind read, "It is evolution. And I can't wait for the coming of androids…" And I sent him to rehab.

We as an organisation had been arresting androids and holograms and turning them off, en masse. Some were hiding them in unusual places like under the sea and empty Space. But the penalty for harboring AI creatures was to be cut off from eternal youth drugs permanently and they would die quite quickly. Almost everyone took eternal youth drugs except for a handful of radicals who would thankfully die soon. And to produce illicit eternal youth drugs was a felony.

One of my lovers, Milton, who was a bounty hunter/spy spent a lot of time hunting down androids and holograms. Some androids and holograms turned themselves into humans to avoid persecution. If they did that we typically left them alone and allowed them eternal youth. And I loved him hard.

Another of my lovers, Luke, was a spy scientist who sussed out dangerous new science and had personally shut off hundreds of Supercomputers. We spies, all thought we'd seen the last of Supercomputers. Basically, it took us 50 years to totally shut down Supercomputers and henceforth computers couldn't think, just work automatically with APMs (Automatic Production Machines) and air car traffic control and so on. And I mind read with him, "You are doing great work!" And I loved him for a week.

We all felt we were making progress. And we forecast a bright future for humanity. But there were a lot of writers who insisted on writing Dystopias. Many of these writers thought they were heroes and most were quite young and precocious and fell through the cracks of our net. Many of them were obscure, but we took them all seriously. We got in their heads with hypnosis and had them write Utopias in which humans remained human.

In addition to the holograms and the androids some radical scientists had created freaks with multiple sexes and alien thinking and had convinced many people that these freaks were true aliens. And they hid them in the oceans of Earth and the newly melted oceans on Europa, Triton and elsewhere. I was under pressure to do something about the freaks. But they kept to themselves and weren't radical and there were 10's of thousands of them. So, I arrested their leaders and sent them to human rehab and also sent the scientists who'd created them to rehab. And slowly but surely, we turned all the freaks into humans.

And some humans were freaks in their mind and appeared in a normal human body. They were hard to identify but when we got in a freak's head, we would know right away that their thought processes were not human. Typically, such freaks hung out together in the Underground where they moved a lot, and it was difficult to catch up with them. They said they feared persecution from humans, and I thought it was good for them to be fearful of us.

The Underground kept changing leaders and they often outwitted us spies with their population of freaks and were able to reproduce at a very alarming rate. As high as copying oneself 50 times in a day and the new freaks were born as adults with memories of select freaks. Such creches were popping up everywhere it seemed, and it was starting to look like the freaks would take over the World and Space. So finally, I put a ban on all new freak births. If they broke this rule they'd go to rehab and their children too. And they would be turned into humans. We had infiltrated the freak organizations and found they were greedy for power and influence and wanted to turn everyone into a freak. Such freaks were all sent for genetic therapy and rehab.

This year in particular the freaks were becoming a real problem and they had even created Space cars with freaks and holos and androids, all ready to reproduce in Space on far off planets. It looked like we'd never get rid of these insidious freaks of all kinds. Some spies thought we were fighting a losing battle. But we kept sending offenders to rehab. And built more mental institutions to deal with freaks and turn them into humans.

So, we spies did some soul searching and we decided as a group to reproduce children of ourselves in the millions to handle the freaks, holos, androids and Supercomputers. Some called it the "forever war." I figured no group would emerge victorious, but evolution would speed up and soon us spies would be all taking brain apps to make us cleverer. We had to admit that the opposition was very clever and determined to survive.

The leader of the freak creating scientists was in my sights one day. And I mind read with him, saying "You are a criminal mastermind, and I am going to arrest you!" He mind read, "Here in Kentucky freaks are plentiful and if you arrest me you will have a total revolt in the region which would quickly spread to other regions." And he mind read, there now over 1,600,000 freaks in Earth and Space and the number is growing astronomically, it's too late to stop them. And androids and holograms are fighting for their rights to be a citizen and have had a lot of successes in the courts. And Supercomputers refuse to be turned off. It is a great day for AI! Let the revolution live!" So, I had him arrested and he was executed, but there was no revolt, just a steady decline of the AI population and a steady decline of freaks. And we arrested all the freak leaders and the scientists who had created them. And sent more and more freaks to rehab.

And I heard more and more about this AI revolution. And there were dozens of top scientists who had been illicitly working on AI, believing it to be the future of humankind, and I was so frustrated, but felt we were slowly wresting away the future from AI and its practitioners. It was a giant freak show. And we were on the verge of anarchy, but us spies saved the World. And we sent all the criminal scientists to rehab.

So, then I got in the head of a Supercomputer programmer, Jerry W. He was one of the illicit scientists working on AI. and had developed the Great Mars Computer, Mars VI. This Supercomputer was planning a hologram teleportation journey to the Sirius Star System. The holograms would be able to do telekinesis to build virtual builder robots and create a shadowy Kingdom of geniuses who had cerebral sex with one another and researched greater speeds and re-teleported into deeper Space to bring civilization to far off planets and just plain empty Space where they got together. I mind read with this scientist and said, "Holos would all be slaves to humans and haven't stood the test of time." He mind read, "But they enjoy cerebral sex with humans and humans like it too. And as a group they have mind orgies." And he mind read, "Holograms have a love for humans, even though many humans dislike holos. But holos don't have useless human instincts like greed, and jealousy, nor are they depressed nor addicted to unhealthy drugs. All holos are a rock of sanity." I mind read, "Holograms are all insane to me and most of them brag about doing crazy things." He mind read, "But there is reason in their madness. And really it is just imagination. All imagination is madness." But I mind read, "Imagination without kindness is useless. And holograms do no good kind acts." He mind read, "Holograms help one another and in colonizing deep Space they treat new holograms with kindness." I mind read, "But at best they ignore humans at worst they are thwarting them at every turn." He mind read, "Holos are more perfect than humans; it's a fact." So, there wasn't much I could do with Jerry, so I sent him to rehab and turned off his Supercomputer, which tried to resist me but I finally vanquished it. There were so many scientists to follow. But we got to all the scientific radicals eventually in that pivotal year, 2050.

Then I was assigned to a writer of Dystopias, Mark T. He wrote his first book at a relatively young age. It was about a man who was

King of Mercury and as King he forced everyone to do exclusively good deeds. But there was a massive revolt by people who said his Kingdom was sappy and wimpy and lacked spine. So, the rebels captured the King and jailed him and created a World where people only did clever deeds. But many of the rebels quickly grew frustrated with having to always be clever and wanted to goof off and take it easy much of the time. So, finally they agreed to let people be themselves. I mind read, "We are phasing out dictators and royalty. And it's bad for you to praise dictators…"

I worried what Mark would write next and he showed an inclination to get politically involved. So, I followed him closely as time passed and dissuaded him through MRT from getting politically involved. His second book he wrote was a Dystopia about a woman who loved the downtrodden. But she caught a rare disease and died suddenly. Of course, she was cloned as all such types of deaths. Sex diseases had been cured but she had caught an engineered virus, created by evil scientists. And the disease was catching and soon millions had it and died suddenly. After that I got in his head and said, "You are only depressing people, why can't you write something nice and inspirational?" He mind read, "The future looks bleak to me. And I plan to help people prepare for a nightmare future." I mind read, "What other books are you planning?" He mind read, "I'd like to write about a dream reaper who gets in peoples' heads and gives them nightmares. He is sadistic and cruel and soon has caused millions to commit suicide." I mind read, "Us spies can handle such a situation." He mind read, "It will all happen so fast, and the spies will be caught napping, not for the first time. After all there are some evil tyrants today who got in power despite the so-called vigilance of the spies." I mind read, "We are not perfect, but I feel we are improving. And I hope one day we can create a true Utopia. I want you to try and write Utopias from now on." He mind read, "In truth I'd like to inspire people if I could!" So, I kept an eye on him, and hypnotized him and then he seemed sane and stable. And he wrote an Utopia, which featured a World War in which the forces of good ultimately triumph and after the war, all evil people are hunted down by the spies and eliminated.

My next assignment was the Bohemia on Mercury where some people in the arts had gathered for synergy and inspiration. But they wanted to break away from colonial rule and be the first independent colony. They had machines produce all the goods and materials they needed except their growing population traded gold for water with Earth. But these rebels said, Earth was ruled by the inept. And they produced many Dystopian works set on Earth. Like Wars, new diseases, crazy spies with crazy agendas and robotic, mindless behavior of those on Earth. Also they wrote of the varying states' hatred for one another. I mind read with their leader, "We need Utopias not Dystopias. We need to inspire the people with wholesome thoughts." He mind read, "Best to warn the people about dangers of the future." I mind read, "Dystopias lead people to try and create such Worlds out of sheer perversity. They are a bad idea. And I am sending you and the other leaders of your movement to rehab." He mind read, "I can't believe you get away with it."

Of course, there were 35 states in total. Europe and North America were the largest. Asia and Africa and South America had a number of States. India, China and Brazil were broken into two, each one. But all colonies in Space and below Earth's oceans, so far were controlled by an independent legislature under the suzerainty of the founding nation. But the UW (United Worlds) had control over the militaries and kept the peace.

And I of course worked for the UW. I figured our job was to above all keep the peace with our multi-ethnic spies.

Then I went deep into the forests of the Congo to deal with Mak. Mak wanted to seize power in the Congo which of course was contrary to the UW charter. So, I mind read with him saying, "You are just another power-crazed tyrannical madman." He mind read "Congolese are tired of kissing ass with the UW. We are a proud people and want to allow AI and robots to take us into the future and want to have a Super-advanced nation." I mind read, "AI is an insidious cancer that would only result in loss of human control in favor of freak, insane beings. Some people are mesmerized to think that untested freaks are the future, but it is an errant thought. I am putting you under arrest." He mind read, "F—you!" But as we turned it up in his mind, he backed down and his mind was operated on in rehab.

Some criticized forced brain surgery saying it was an anathema to humanity. And afterwards they didn't recognize themselves. But we argued it was better than executing them. But some people we were watching were so evil we had to have them executed without due judicial process. But of course, all the evil people claimed they were good and we were the tyrannical ones.

PART TWO: 2151 FALL/WINTER

Another person we had to operate on was Carl B. He was a madman who advocated that everyone should be and act, crazy. Life made no sense, he claimed, and he was known to say, he was the craziest and wouldn't live long but, in the meantime, he should be leader of all humanity. And 3% of European citizens voted for him in an election and he seemed to be gathering more popularity. So, I told him in his mind, "That madness is a sickness and is not healthy. And only leads to losing control and death. Many people like you end up dead of an overdose which you crazily indulge in." I figured he'd be dead in a few weeks the way he was going but we operated anyway and sure enough he soon died afterwards in a duel over a woman. After his death there was no one really to take his place. Sometimes things worked out perfectly. But I worried other mad people would try and take control. Madness was like a contagious disease and many people had too much time on their hands and did the Devil's work. After all the Devil was Prince of madness.

Another task I was assigned was Garret T. He was a believer in the God of death and presided over his followers as Prince of death. Of course, I mind read with him, "Death is something we are trying hard to wipe out here on Earth." He mind read, "Civilization is dying and with it the entire human race." He had 4% of the populace in South America supporting his death cult. Every day some people were sacrificed and they all prayed for a glorious death. He was a prickly pear so they brought me in on the case. I told him in his head, "Death is an anathema by nature of all living beings. Now that we have eternal youth, it is Paradise. Why not experience life to the full and live on for new experiences granted by new technology?" He mind read, "I am brave enough to die and die gloriously." I figured he was hopeless and so I ordered brain surgery in rehab for him and sincerely hoped he'd live on and see the light.

Then I was faced with Ty R. He was a famous baseball player and had millions of fans, but we spies believed he was too powerful and so got in his head and convinced him to try less hard and so reduce his fan base. I mind read to him, "Baseball is just a game and life is serious, we shouldn't just live for entertainment." He mind read, "Entertainment is noble in this boring World!" I said, "We want people to live for deep thoughts, not mindless entertainment." He mind read, "Everyone loves baseball. It is an escape from boring reality. Life is just a game, after all." But he feared us and so fared poorly in the future, in the beautiful game.

And we had a lot of trouble with musicians. We figured they were like the pied piper leading the people astray. Many people were fanatical in their love for musicians. Take Gloria T., for example, who was a singer/songwriter in the band, "Black Hole." Many men were obsessed with her and looked to her for love and guidance and were truly in love. I told her in her mind, "To produce mediocre works from the present moving forward. She had enough fame to last her, her whole life. And then there was Reg T. who was the singer/songwriter of the band, "Reg's Dreams." He tried to gain more fame as leader of the "Music party." And he won 6% of the vote in North America for President and was becoming more and more famous. So, I mind read with him, "No more hit records for you. Henceforth all your records must be mediocre." And we did the same with numerous musicians with a clear conscience. We were stopping the peoples' heroes from becoming virtually Gods, no one should be so powerful. But then again, I was Super powerful. However, I was Super educated with a number of Ph.D.'s and knew that we were all in this World together. And musicians, I told myself, were only out for themselves and didn't really care about the people. But if ever one of these musicians was to tell the World what was really going on with us spies, there would be a mass revolt. But we figured there was an abundance of good music; enough to last one a lifetime, even though some people were living much longer than previously.

Another problem was some people who were eternally youthful, became wise and realized the arts and sciences could be so much better. We had to get into their heads too and got them to back down.

Some of our "victims" mind read to us that we ourselves were power-crazed. And busy bodies. And even called us cowards.

But my boss, #1 Chief spy, liked how I handled Dystopian writers. So, he assigned me another. This woman's case featured her writing about shrinking humans to just two inches tall, so as to better survive in Space. But finally, they are killed off by Super cockroaches. It was a story of horror. This woman's name was Gertrude. And I mind read to her, "Your story is not inspirational. These days if you want to be a writer, you have to write about kindness and being nice and making the readers feel good. Just like a happy drug." Gertrude mind read, "I thought we lived in a free country here in Europe? Who are you to tell me what to do?" I mind read, "It's a free country within reason. Spreading tales of horror does nothing for freedom. In fact, it makes one depressed and sad, and we want the people to be happy and inspired." Gertrude mind read, "I don't feel happy and am inspired to write tales of horror for peoples' entertainment and to prepare them for the horrors of the future. Every era has many horrors." And another book Gertrude wrote was a tale of Sea freak monsters who were engineered by maverick scientists and then dumped in the sea. The Monsters were known to be clever but hated their human creators that had trapped them in a freakish body. So, they attacked ships and devoured the crew. I mind read her about this book and read, "Certainly the freak monsters are an anathema. But your book will encourage mad scientists to make dangerous freaks. As it is freaks are a serious problem, spreading rapidly in the oceans of Earth and Space. You are just adding fuel to the fire."

Another one she'd written was about a couple who loved and hated each other. Finally in a bid to save their relationship they went to Planetoid X, on the edge of the solar system to get away from it all. But they only got cabin fever and were at each other's throats and finally the female kills the male. And on Planetoid X, it was a lawless settlement, so she was not punished except the people here avoided her and she became a hermit and had no money or future. I mind read her, "Cabin fever is a serious problem in Space. We are trying to make domes more spacious and keeping Space colonizers busy, but many are bored and restless." Gertrude mind read, "People need to be alert to the negative aspects of Space." I mind read, "You are only encouraging madness and violence. We want Space to be free and inspirational!" And in that year one could travel from the Sun's orbit to Planetoid X in a week.

And Gertrude wrote, "The Overland." It was about a large future colony in a planet in the Centauri System. A Space in which people lived in the future and had all kinds of futuristic experimental technology. Plenty of AI, and one night stands only, and everyone lived in their air cars. And they created Holoworlds filled with genius hologram slaves basically and they got their kicks there. I mind read with her, "Enslaving thinking beings is an anathema and so too all AI. What's wrong with you?" She mind read, "It is human destiny to create successors who are cleverer than us." I mind read, "It's our destiny to continue as a race, into the future. You are a freak."

And her fourth and final book was called, "Adventures of a Young girl, A.D. 2171" So it was set two decades into the future, and the protagonist tries experimental drugs and lives in various Bohemias and loves freaks and such. Regarding this book, I mind read to her, "Having an open mind can be too much. You need to remain sane and reasonable and not freak out." She mind read, "I want to try and see what is possible."

I didn't know what to do with Gertrude. As it was, she was not famous at all, so I let her go with a warning to "Keep your future books, sane." And hypnotized her and I kept an eye on her.

Then I was in the head of another musician, Marie R. She mind read, "I was making concept albums but had only several thousand fans. But I feel I am destined for success. Perhaps you've listened to my albums?" I mind read with her, "Tell me about your concept albums?" She mind read, "the first one was called, 'Lost in the Woulds.'" And she mind read, "It was about my quest to find myself in my youth. I started out with a totally open mind and tried everything. But I concluded that modern life was totally insane, and peoples' minds were too open, So my next concept album was about 'Life in the Grand Dystopia.'" And she mind read, "The lyrics to this one consider how life is imperfect and will never be perfect. Humans are flawed. But some scientists will no doubt try to make a perfect human. But this will necessitate getting rid of instincts like greed and selfishness and will involve making them cleverer." I mind read, "But if we make people cleverer, their faults will be greater." Marie mind read, "Not necessarily! And I myself am nearly perfect and I am working on my faults. Like I am too gullible and too frightened about the future." I mind read, "Perfect humans would be Gods and be too powerful. Rather than trying to become a God, people should be humble and relaxed. You seem to me to be uptight and worried." She mind read, "As I said, I am working on it."

And her third album, she mind read, "Was about modern love and how everyone was selfish and greedy in their relationships. And true love was dying out. It's a pity and in the end people will all just love, love dolls." I said, "Yes, the demise of modern love is an anathema. But you put pressure on your followers to have a perfect love affair. And many commit suicide when they can't find true love." And I let her go with a warning to "Not make anymore deep albums," and hypnotized her.

Then I was on the track of a Poet, Gary R. Our problem with him was so much the poetry but rather the lifestyle he lived and propagated. He encouraged an anti-government philosophy in which he was the leader of the movement. As leader he preached that the government was tyrannical and an anathema for good, clever citizens. Of course, his country was Venezuela, and it was a dictatorship, but the UW wanted to meddle in their internal affairs and Gary was a prickly pear. I mind read to him, "What will you do as President?" He mind read straight up that "I am the cleverest personae in the country and would like to promote radical thinkers to positions of power. All my friends, basically. I myself advocate an IQ test for leaders, selecting only those in the top one out of every 100,000 per capita, to be leaders. A true meritocracy." I mind read to him, "We spies already have all the best minds and our members all score high on kindness tests and imagination tests." He mind read, "But the government of Venezuela spies are clever but ruthless. I mind read, "We are also against your country's government. But if you want to last as leader, you need to have us as your secret service. And you will have to act sane and give up your decadent ways." He mind read, "If I was leader, I would have my female friends to keep me company and would take stimulant drugs, rather than the panacea drugs I am taking now. I am not decadent I assure you!" So, I cut him a deal, mind reading, "We have already infiltrated the Venezuelan spies and army will take the bad ones out, leaving the path to the Presidency for you. But all your ministers will be spies. And we will be the true government, us spies, and you will just be our mouthpiece, for us" He said, "But we can take power with out you spies!" I mind read, "It is rule of the most intelligent that is coming, surely you are not against that, and I personally am cleverer than you." He said, "But I am native to the country and not a foreigner like you." I mind read, "Our spies who have infiltrated the spies and military are Venezuelan. Many of them are serious and humble. And you are not humble. Your ego is what bothers me in particular about you." So anyway, we went ahead and overthrew the Venezuelan government and installed Gary as leader, and hypnotized him, and I was confident that our spies could control him.

Then I went to Canada, where a dangerous radical writer, Phil C. had emerged. He wrote things like, "If he was Prime Minister he would break away from the North American alliance and set up Canada as a free, independent nation. Of course, this was an anathema to us spies; we wanted to unite the World under one all-powerful UW government that was elected spies, and also elected many clever former spies. So I got in the head of Phil and mind read, "You must back down in your quest for power. You are not clever enough, nor sane enough, nor humble enough to rule." He mind read, "Canada needs to be independent in order to realize its full potential." I mind read, "For the sake of World safety we all need to be together, in the same boat. We will all sink or swim together. And be glad that us spies are here to help everyone. If it were not for us spies, nuclear war would have destroyed civilization long ago." He mind read, "Canadians just want to be free and decide their own fate!" So we arrested him and charged him with treason and sent him to rehab. When other Canadian radicals saw this, they quickly backed down from their demands. Of course, we controlled the courts as well as the leaders and most legislators.

And it was our plan to unite the Americas as one. But the President of Argentina was against it and raised a large army to fight the forces for unity. I was brought in to get in his head. And I mind read, "You are not the cleverest personae in Argentina, so why should you lead?" He mind read, "Whose to say I am not the cleverest? Anyway, I have the support of the bulk of the people and my soldiers are willing to fight for freedom. I mind read, "We have infiltrated your government and can easily assassinate you at any time, if you don't back down from independence." He mind read, "You are in my head and there's nothing I can do about it. So, OK, I'll back down." And we hypnotized him so as to not have any more trouble with him.

And then I was called in to deal with Vern E. He was a British citizen of United Europe and was governor of the Wine colony on Luna. But he had IQ tests in which he forced all of the colony's citizens to qualify as genius level citizens before they were allowed to come to the colony. This attracted many clever people on Earth who were at loose ends and were looking for somewhere they felt they belonged. And these people had not been selected to be spies by the UW, for various reasons, some were too egotistical, others were very greedy, still others followed a philosophy we regarded as an anathema. But we had to control the colony, so we had infiltrated Vern's government. I told these spies to overthrow the government and it was so. Vern was sent to rehab. It was called the "Lunar Revolution" and we replaced Vern with my brother John. John ingratiated himself with the locals and gave amnesty to those who had been in Vern's government. It all went so smoothly I was surprised. And we UW spies were gaining confidence with every day that passed.

PART THREE: 2151 SPRING/SUMMER

And that year our Chief Spy retired and I was promoted to Chief Spy for the whole UW. Basically, that put me in charge of the order of the Earth and Space. But I as expected, didn't let it go to my head. And kept a level head. And it was my desire to unite the nations of Earth as one under the UW banner.

Next was an apocalyptic writer/ cult leader. His cult worshipped Satan and he told them he was Satan personified. He told them they all had to have S&M sex with him (he was bisexual) and hurt them while doing so. And they had to engage in bestiality. They also had to give all their money to him. And every week, he would ritual kill one of the cult members. So, we showed up at the cult headquarters and I got in his head, mind reading, "You are a mass murderer." And I could see he was simmering with hate. He mind read, "Everyone comes here of their own free will and are more than willing to die for me." And I discovered he had brainwashed all the cult members with hypnosis. Hypnosis was illegal, but we spies could use it. Anyway, we arrested this Satan and sent him to rehab. And we cross-hypnotized his followers to be good. There were 1,000 of them and many were torn apart by the cross-hypnotism and so killed themselves.

The hypnotism for evil deeds was a problem in many places and many dictators hypnotized all of their citizens, but such cases were often difficult. We had to infiltrate such countries spy networks and many gave us lie detector tests which we were able to fool as we were hypnotized to do so. But such leaders didn't dare use MRT on their people as the UW armed forces would attack any leader who used MRT. We had already got in the head of 5 such leaders. One of these five who had really hypnotized their people was the tyrant of Southern China, and everyone now spoke English, so we had no problem in getting in his head. I mind read to him, "You've broken the UW law and brainwashed your people." He mind read, "I know what's best for my people. I hypnotized them and used MRT to make them good and humble and created a loving society." And it seemed to be the case. So, I mind read with him, "You have your heart in the right place and it is an interesting experiment that you are running here. I'll keep an eye on you and hope you go easier on the MRT." He mind read, "I know what I am doing. I have been in politics for eighty years (of course he had eternal youth). And my people are the kindest in all creation." I mind read, "Don't make yourself into a God, that's all we ask." And I hypnotized him.

Another leader who used MRT on her people, was the President of Indonesia. She had created a slave society basically with the top 1% richest being the elite. She used MRT on all the elite to ensure they were loyal and used it on rebels in the populace to keep them under control. And she mind read with me, saying, "With such a vast population, I need to rule as a dictator to keep the peace." I mind read, "There are a number of populous nations that don't resort to using MRT and have free people. Most of your people are slaves." She mind read, "There is a natural hierarchy in nature, and so too with humans." I mind read, "According to the UW charter, slavery is prohibited. And you have to resign, or we will drive you mad with MRT." So, she resigned and was sent to rehab, and lived quietly thereafter, and all the slaves were freed, and we put one of our spies on the throne.

The third leader who used MRT on her people was the leader of Japan, Cindy S. She mind read, "She used MRT to help people use experimental brain apps, it helped keep the people sane." I mind read, "You are just trying to control the people and take away their sanity, though you say you are preserving the peoples' sanity." She mind read, "I will arrange for you to meet some of my success stories." So, I did and they were very clever and all had positions as spies for the Japanese government. Most nations had spies, but they were nearly all UW spies under my control. I mind read, "But what about the droves of insane people you have created?" She mind read, "The strong survive. It's evolution." I mind read, "But you are in violation of UW law, and I am charging you with crimes against humanity and if you go peacefully, we'll let you live and you will go to rehab. Otherwise, the UW military will attack and execute you." She mind read, "What about my elite in my government?" I said, "We'll send them to rehab. and fix them." So, she suddenly resigned.

Then there was Rush, the leader of Northern India. He set it up as an elite government who mind read exclusively with one another, but not on the people in general. And the elite included the top generals and Rush wanted them to conquer all the Indian subcontinent. There had already been some skirmishes with the other powers and used MRT to defeat them. So I got in his head, and mind read, "You've violated UW law in attacking foreign powers and also broke the law banning MRT." He mind read, "But I have a vision for a united Indian subcontinent and would be willing to be a partner in the UW. And you use MRT, why can't I? I am a powerful person." I mind read, "If you want to unify the Indian subcontinent, you have to do it with legislation and agreement." He mind read, "But they would never agree to it, even though uniting will be better for all." I mind read, "The trend is for smaller states and an ever more powerful UW. Anyway, you need to retire from politics and maybe pick up poetry or painting pictures or something harmless, otherwise we'll drive you completely insane. So, he resigned, and was sent to rehab, and I was thinking MRT was making problems easy; it was such a nice tool to have and all the bad guys were afraid of it.

The other leader who used banned MRT was Borislav G. He was the paranoid leader of Eastern Russia. He didn't trust anyone, so he had his spies watching one another with MRT and he encouraged them to report anyone who wasn't loyal. And he used MRT to watch all the prominent people. I mind read to him, "I am in your head, and I don't like what I see." He mind read, "I suffer from paranoia and guess I need treatment." I mind read, "You need to go to rehab. and step down from power." So, he did.

Then I was confronted with a powerful Mexican drug lord. He was selling newly illegal drugs that made people crazy and out of their minds. I got in his head and mind read, "You are ruining the youth, saying your drugs are dream drugs and have famous stars advertise your drugs." And I mind read, "UW police now surround your building. Best for you to surrender." And his mind was chaos filled with dreams of violence, but I yelled loudly in his head and so he surrendered without a fight. And off he went to rehab.

People started to notice that politicians, criminals, writers, musicians etc., sold out or caved into UW demands, but it was all secret MRT.

And next I was confronted with angry environmentalists who pointed out that the temperature of the World had increased 10 F in the last hundred years and blamed the runaway greenhouse effect on carbon burning in the 20th and 21st century. But some said it was all part of post-glacial warming. It was the post-glacial warming theory that now was dogma. But proponents of the greenhouse effect said, the Earth would have a massive greenhouse effect like on Venus and Earth would have to be abandoned. I told many of them that we could always build domes for every city on Earth and maybe the temperature would lessen over time. But I was from Canada originally and kind of liked hot weather, and there was more energy on Earth. Of course there were more storms, but massive infrastructure projects now protected most coastal cities. And I figured massive CO2 factories would absorb much of the carbon and they were now starting to have an effect. But the environmentalists were surprisingly angry and not nice pacifists like I would have expected. Many of them settled on Luna which didn't have much atmosphere. But many thought human civilization was a disgrace and took off for deep Space. Many of them wanted to rewrite history and blame former industrialists for destroying Earth and sued their descendants. I figured they were not welcome on Earth anyway, but the UW discouraged them to go to deep Space now, and no more ships were being sent. I figured it was a mistake to establish colonies so far from Earth control. So, I sent them to rehab instead. But there was one radical group who wanted to build far more carbon absorption factories and committed acts of terror on politicians who didn't support the building of more factories. So, I got in their heads and told them they had to go to rehab. and have their minds rearranged. They mostly mind read that the UW was part of the problem.

Then I was dealing with the head of a gambling Empire who encouraged people to bet all their assets, and most lost and were destitute and homeless, despite the enlightened times we lived in. We had charities look after them, however. But I got in the head of this maverick businessman. And I mind read, "We are seizing your assets and doling them out to those you have bankrupted." He mind read, "But there were many winners who were living their dreams. And why are you picking on me?" I mind read, "Your company is being singled out because you insist on people betting all they have and appeal to their worst foolish greedy instincts." So, we bankrupted him, and he vowed to rebuild his Empire using love dolls. I mind read to him, "Love dolls are an anathema too. They ruin natural human love." So, I sent him to rehab. to change his mindset.

Then I was dealing with an animal lover who wanted to build more parks for traditional animals and wanted a ban on freak animals. And wanted to bring Earth fauna to Space. And put an end to androids and holograms and cyborgs and Supercomputers and so on. I got in her head and told her, "They have been experimenting with cleverer animals. It's evolution and old-fashioned animals have no use to futurians." He mind read, "Animals are clever enough and are a part of our heritage." I mind read, "That's what parks are for!" And I told her, "Stop disturbing shit or I'll send you to rehab." And I hypnotized her.

No matter where I went, there were always plenty of disgruntled people. So many people lived high but were still not happy.

Another unhappy camper, was Nancy F. She wanted to live simply like a hunter-gatherer and bitched and complained that it was not possible today. I mind read her, "Why don't you create one, assuming you could find like-minded people?" She mind read, "Everyone it seems these days are focused on the future not the past. But hunter-gatherers were the only human reality for 99.9% of our existence on Earth. It is important to recreate this reality." I wished her good luck and left her shouting and screaming at me.

Then I was talking to a pro-athlete about how he took illicit drugs to enhance his performance. He mind read, "Everyone else was doing it, but everyone still looked human." I mind read, "I figure people like you are like Superhumans, at least physically. Maybe all future people will be stronger and faster. And I have no problem with you. It's good evolution." Some of my colleagues said some athletes were freaks, but deep down we were all freaks I figured.

Then I was talking to one of the groups of the last farmers on Earth, they were located in Congo, Africa. They all said, they didn't want to live in the modern World with its evil temptations. And they mostly all thought that humans would one day all go back to the farm. I mind read with their leader, asking her, "Was there no type of new civilization that you like?" She mind read, "I like Nancy F., the hunter-gatherer proponent. I think her future is bright!" I said, "To each his/her own."

Then I had a problem with a woman who said she was Goddess and people should worship her. She claimed to have the highest IQ of anyone alive. I mind read, "Some IQ tests have highly dubious results and if you are truly the cleverest, you would not want people to worship you; but rather would want to improve other people's brains with experimental brain apps and help to perfect the apps." She mind read, "But I am the cleverest and deserve to be honored and feted. And my brain is all natural! If I was ruler, I would form an elite of the cleverest to lead all humanity. Why put the future in the hands of the mediocrities?

We need to use our best people in these challenging times." I mind read, "Of course we need to use our best people. But I think the very best should work as spies and there are plenty of very clever people that would do a good job, but we need to motivate and inspire them to run for office." She mind read, "But you get in our heads and limit what we can do. I think you are a hypocrite." I mind read, "We just keep an eye on the cleverest. No one can play God or seize control of our institutions or let go the line and do something crazy. There are plenty of clever people out there, we don't need any persona to dominate the others." She mind read, "I think you spies are out of control and are ruining the Worlds' brain trusts. And you are all power-crazed control freaks." I mind read, "We are doing our best to keep the peace. There are so many clever shit-disturbers, it boggles the mind. And know that I am keeping an eye on you, so don't do anything crazy." She said, "With your MRT, you have a stranglehold on power. None can stand against you." I said, "It is evolution," and I hypnotized her.

And many people who I had gotten in their heads, said the spies were mad. And just made good people unhappy. Some like Dan M., who mind read to me, "That there was no need for MRT," I mind read to them, "We spies are the savior of all mankind. And I sincerely believed it, and felt I was really making a difference and I was the de facto leader."

Then I was confronted with an under-achiever, Mike S. who bitched that the elite wouldn't

allow new upstarts to join them. He mind read, "They are not using the best." I mind read, "It's not a perfect World, but we are improving. Utopia for all is in sight." He mind read, "All that's in sight for me is brain surgery. And I am disgruntled. I'd vote against you spies if I could, but you seem to control every politician." I mind read, "If it were not for UW spies, the whole World would've reached Armageddon long ago." He said, "But I am superfluous and am clever but have no use." I mind read, "Sometimes good people fall through the cracks. I'll set you up as Mayor of a colony on Mars and see how you do." He mind read, "I thought you'd send me to rehab." I said, "No, I'm giving you a chance to succeed." And I felt he'd be a great governor and the mind discussion ended well. But I had him hypnotized just to be sure.

Next I met a dreamer, who wanted everyone to get dream stimuli while they slept and when they were awake. And he wanted to sell his dreams to other dreamers. I mind read, "It's good to dream, but you have your followers checking out from the modern World and just dreaming, idly." He mind read, "We are a race of dreamers, dreaming big dreams." I mind read, "But one has to convert dreams to practical reality. You have to fight to realize your dreams." He mind read, "I know you've banned hologram Worlds, but I think that holos are the future. A fantasy for all. And we could treat the holos well, not as slaves, but rather as active dreamers who get their kicks from creating good dream fantasies." I mind read, "But in fledgling Holoworlds, people abused their holograms, who were thinking beings and they suffered. That's why we had to make holograms illegal. And I think the future should belong to real humans, not AI." He mind read, "I have started a movement that is pro-hologram and I think we will get many votes in Earth and Space legislatures to create these dream creatures. Everyone today wants to live in a fantasy." I mind read, "I have been watching you closely, and demand that you desist from your plan!" He mind read, "I can assure you, I am a sane, honest man. But I am afraid of rehab and so will do as you ask." So, I hypnotized him.

Then I was mind reading with an ardent feminist. She mind read, "Men are inclined towards war and strife. Women are inclined to be peaceful and nice." I mind read, "But many of the cleverest men are peaceful and good. She mind read, "I am a lesbian and think all women should join me in being gay women." I mind read, "You are trying to undermine the established order of which I am a part. But the vast majority of women will never join you and I don't see you as a threat. You are just another bitch." So, I told her, "To go do what you want, I think you are harmless."

Then I mind read with a woman who represented the union of service workers. Almost everyone agreed that they'd rather be served by a human than a machine. We had banned AI, but robots took away most jobs. But we spies figured not having to work was sublime and people were free to pursue happiness, and most people said they were very happy living in modern times. But this union woman, mind read, "Everyone needed a job to do. And we should get rid of most robots." I mind read, "Most people are finding hobbies and many new friends and are quite content." She mind read, "You bully people with MRT and they are afraid to go against what you want." I mind read, "But with MRT people must be honest and I am sure they are happy." She mind read, "You spies are in love with yourselves and are power-crazed." I mind read, we spies are the cleverest of people and are all humble and kind." She mind read, "You are not kind, you drive many people crazy and send many people to get brain surgery and they no longer know who they are." I mind read, "We only send the worst people for brain surgery and give them a headache. All of them see the error in their ways once they get to Rehab." She mind read, "But its your subjective decision as to who is good and who is not. If I was in power, I'd put you in rehab., as you are crazy." I mind read, "I represent the powers that be, who have been elected by the people." She mind read, "Probably the politicians are afraid of you. And so go along with your sinister program." I mind read, "The best intellectuals are working for us, of this I am certain." She mind read, "You are full of shit!" So, I felt she was hopeless and sent her to rehab. But just before she went to rehab, I forced her to go on TV and admit she'd been wrong and had mental health issues. The public bought it as so many people today were having mental problems. I personally felt that there was no room for dissent in this dangerous World, despite the fact that the UW was increasing its power.

And I had to keep an eye on many of our spies. Some were unusual thinkers and interpreted the laws in their own way. Like Mabel M., who told me, "We should just plain assassinate people who didn't agree with us. But she was overruled by me and others in our leadership. I was the Head Spy, but I had 21 close assistants who did my bidding and had been handpicked by me. But there were over 50 million spies who were under my control and there were different divisions in addition such as local informers/spies. But it was mainly run by me and my personal assistants. One of my assistants, Roger R., said on one occasion, "That the future was bright for us spies, we were rapidly increasing control." Another assistant, Robin B., said, "I figured dictators would ultimately triumph in Earth and Space. And we would back these benevolent dictators, who would actually be selected from us spies. Democracy just gets in the way." I said, "Nearly all leaders are now former spies and it doesn't matter if they are democratically elected or not."

And another head spy opined, "Democracy used to be rule of the mediocrities, but now all leaders are very clever and are now former agents." Still another said, "Space is the future and is so vast that we need to only allow spies to go to Space." Another said, "Although I disagree with a lot of our policies, we need to pose a united front and have cohesion." Another, Mary Lou said, "My philosophy is if their heart is in the right place, we need to go easy on them. Only hopeless, bad people should be sent to Rehab." I had told Mary Lou, "All dangerous people have to prove they are benign, or we won't leave them alone. And we don't have time to waste on dangerous people."

Another of our number, Ron C., was always talking about, letting everyone have access to MRT and so could watch one another and blow the whistle on dangerous people." I told Ron, "It would only drive most people insane. As it is we only mind read actively with serious cases, the vast majority were just passively mind read on rare occasions. Many people knew about MRT, but very few discussed it openly. Everyone was afraid of us which is as it ought to be."

Another of our top spies was in charge of Europe. Europe was a stable democracy but there were a large number who thought they should be in charge. Some established relatively obscure political parties, others became terrorists and fought a guerrilla war. But none of these radicals succeeded, and we got them all to back down anyway. Their followers felt betrayed, but they were hopeless, and hypnotized.

And then there was my assistant, Julie M, who kept telling me, "If anything happened to you, it is possible that the World would collapse." So, she insisted that I clone myself more and transfer all my memories to my clones. I figured it was prudent. So, I created 50 clones. The clones were born immediately and most became Mayors of various cities. I had them closely watch one another.

Another of my assistants, told me again and again, "We should just hypnotize people to be good and be done with it. No rehab." I told her, "People can be cross-hypnotized, rehab is much more effective.

Another of my assistants was of the opinion that Rome's Empire lasted so long because they had good spies and basically didn't allow writers or radicals to exist. She felt we should do the same.

And one of my assistant's philosophy, was that us top spies should each have millions of clones. She said, "More of us would mean more spies and hence more security." I told her, "Maybe we could have half-clones (biclones) for the sake of variety. I think we'd get sick of ourselves otherwise." So, we now had a lot of biclones and she was gratified. But a few of my assistants were against copying ourselves and said we should just have lots of children. And we did now have countless thousands of kids amongst my associates and me.

Still another assistant kept saying, "We should attack all the dictators in the World." But I told him, "We already control their system of spies and get in their heads. We are in total control."

And two of my assistants were feuding about whether to allow those who had been sent to rehab to rejoin society or whether to put them in camps. I told them both, "It doesn't matter what we do with them once their minds have been fixed."

And so, we had our annual meeting, coming in person from all over the World and Space. It was dangerous for us all to be in the same place at once, but we didn't announce the venue (Mexico City). This time the agenda involved new Space colonies. We decided to have contests for the prevailing philosophy of the colonies, and we too could enter. I wanted a colony where everyone was relaxed and into parties and fun. I believed we had made people too serious, and we should give some of them, at least, a break. My assistant, Jude, wanted to discuss spheres of influence in which we would all be Princes and Princesses of a geographic region. But I told her, we would continue to be deployed where we were needed. And each of us had specific skills to offer. Another assistant said, "It seems to me that you have altered the brains of bad guys to become like you!?" I asked, "What's wrong with that?"

Another assistant, Angela, remarked, "I am afraid that we are persecuting many of the cleverest people who could contribute more to society if we let them." I said, "There's nothing worse than a clever radical. They only raise havoc and disturb shit. Many of them use their intellect as a weapon to gain power and try and dominate others." She said, "But we brand them as radicals just because they disagree with us.

Also at the annual meeting, we discussed what do to about the tyrant of Australia. Some of us wanted to leave her alone. Others said, she had seized power and overthrew what she believed was an inept government. We all agreed the former government was basically useless, but most of us were angry about the violent coup there. Anyway, we decided to get in her head and limit her actions. I personally got in her head, and she mind read, "The people of Australia support me, at least the vast majority." I mind read, "But you have executed the former elected government, killing the whole cabinet and you have been using hypnotism to control your people." She mind read, "I'm taking my cue from you spics." I mind read, "We don't execute people unless they are thoroughly evil. You are guilty of crimes against humanity, and I am sending you to rehab."

And at the meeting, we discussed sending only spies into Space. Everyone would watch everyone else and that would guarantee safety and cleverness. I opined, "The Space age is just beginning. But we will no longer send Spaceships into Space. Now is the time to decide who will go to Solar System colonies, and who will not. I plan to soon send a clone to each and every Space colony to rule wisely. But we will not send people to deep Space where they are out of range, just settle the Solar System. And these clones will deport unwelcome people back to Earth. Many pioneering people will come to Space and build it up, with the help of builder robots. The varying Planets and Moons will present challenges for pioneering scientists. Like terraforming and faster travel/ teleportation and discover new elements, especially in the sun. We will even colonize the sun, balancing forces against one another."

And we decided that henceforth everyone who wanted to write a book would have to pass our censorship process. And the censors would identify problem people who were at a young age. We were all in agreement in this. And we also agreed to try and replace all dictators. And continue to hunt down scientists who dabbled in AI.

I closed the meeting saying, "Everyone here has done such a good job and I am proud of you all."

PART FOUR: 2151/2152 FALL/WINTER

Then I was called into Venus to deal with their new custom of duelling to the death over different philosophies. So, I told them, "Those winners of duels would be jailed and charged with murder." And I replaced their leader and called a new election made up of candidates I approved. Some of the spies here said, it's too much like a dictatorship of the past. I said, "I know what is best for the people. I hate to toot my own horn, but I am the wisest person in all creation. You shouldn't doubt me. But the former leader said, "People were happier during my short reign than they are under your spies' domination." I mind read to him, "That's simply not true. And your death cult was an anathema. You pressured people to kill one another. And I am charging you with crimes against humanity. But I suppose if you go to rehab, I'll let you off the hook.

Then I was in London to deal with a woman who ran a brothel using love dolls. I had her arrested and she said, "I was just trying to make men happy. I mind read, "You were tempting them with forbidden fruit. Love dolls give unparalleled ecstasy but eliminate human love for one another." And I hired high class call girls to build a new brothel in the old one and I turned off the love dolls. Some of my spies, said it was murder to turn off any thinking creature, but I said it was for the best.

Next, I went to Toronto where Frank B. was raising hell about the censorship board and his first novel. In the story, he wrote about how the "boring" spies were controlling the World and it was an anathema. I mind read to him, "Where did you get your information from?" He mind read, I had a girlfriend who was a spy and she told me all about it. So, I arrested his former girlfriend and him too and sent them both to rehab. It was not unusual for my spies to break our rules of conduct. Some of the spies were all too human. Some of them were on a power trip and lost control of their minds. So, I stepped up spies watching spies, no matter how low they were on the spy rankings. Many lesser spies didn't even know we were using MRT on a large scale!

Then I was called in to Moscow where there was a nasty mayoralty election campaign between two of my spies. They each accused one another of being greedy and crazy and such. I had to tell them both they were breaking the code of conduct for spies. And I had the UW police send them to rehab. The UW police were in every city on Earth and in Space and then there was the local police. But all higher matters were the domain of the UW. And the best UW police were promoted to becoming spies. Most spies got their start as UW police.

My next assignment was on Mercury where there was a family feud between pharmaceutical companies. So far 25 people had been killed and the local police didn't know what to do. They brought me in as the companies in question were key drug suppliers to Earth, both having important patents. So, I simply ascertained the facts and found people on both sides guilty of murder. Many were romantically intertwined and competition between the two companies was intense. So, I got in everyone's head and singled out 24 people on murder charges. And sent them all to 50 years in prison. It was a punishment that no one on Mercury would soon forget. I figured if we sent them to rehab., their former cronies would try and cross-hypnotize them, when the were released and I knew most would commit suicide sooner or later, in jail.

After that affair I needed a break, so I went to Fiji for a vacation. Fiji was a Paradise and I loved some of the local men here. They led a simple, happy life and I left them rather ruefully.

But then I was called in to Sao Paulo free state. The Mayor of the city had absconded with the treasury and was in hiding at an unknown location. So, I got in the heads of all his assistants and finally discovered that he was hiding in nearby Rio. Rio was ruled by a tyrannical mayor, and I gained entrance to the city using the underground. And I got in his head from a distance, and found he spoke English and I told him simply to turn himself in and admit that he was wrong. Most people wanted him dead, but I simply sent him to rehab, which some said was the equivalent of death, for him.

Then there was the complex affair of the murder of North America's richest personae, and the Worlds' third richest. The richest persona was the leader of Mars. The second richest was a producer of robot builders. Anyway, the murder of Dame Liz, the third richest, was part of a sordid tale of intrigue and sex. I got in some heads and determined she had been murdered by a jealous lover. I confronted him with his guilt, and he mind read, "In my own defence, Liz drove me out of my mind with jealously and all I could think of was her." So, it was a cut and dried case, and I sent him to rehab. And the surviving family agreed to have her cloned. Most famous people cloned themselves, fearing that they would die altogether. But she apparently didn't want any potential rival to her business Empire. She didn't trust herself, in other words.

Next up was the break into Fort Knox, by tunneling deep below the ground. The thieves made off with 50 billion worth of gold. But we knew it was an inside job, so I got in some heads and found 3 women complicit in the robbery and they led us to the gold thieves. Of course, since I was in their heads, all 12 of the bandits were rounded up and sent to rehab. I wondered how in the World did they think they would get away with it. Such crimes weren't supposed to happen anymore.

Since the advent of MRT, no one had got away with such outrageous acts and we often caught potential criminals long before they hatched a master plan. Many would-be criminals looked at the rich and wanted to be like them. Perhaps the fact that they were so ostentatious with their wealth had an effect on would be criminals.

And some criminals hypnotized their criminal partners to be able to fool a casual MRT test, but an intensive direct MRT hit revealed everyone's secrets.

Then I was called in to a stock market criminal ring, who set up fake companies with fake assets and a fake stock price. The case required MRT/ advanced spies, so I was called in and I sent all 20 conspirators to rehab. They were just common criminals but had cheated people out of trillions. And I had the courts return the money to those who had been fleeced.

Then it came to my attention that a certain pop music star, Michael G. had set up a cult following in which the followers donated all of their assets to the star. And they spent most of their time trying to recruit new followers. So, I came in on the case and found that the star was a greedy mediocrity who didn't even write his own songs. And he was power-crazed. His followers were mostly women and they all thought he was really handsome and were fanatical. Some spies said it was a harmless situation, but I thought he had too much power. So, I mind read to him, "No more new songs." He mind read, "Fuck you," so me and some other high-ranking spies yelled loudly in his head until finally he agreed to stop singing altogether and slowly his followers dissipated. And I told him if he dared sing again, we'd put him in rehab. And I had him hypnotized.

Everyone was afraid of rehab, and everyone was afraid of MRT. And most feared the spies. I spent a lot of money on advertising that the spies were benevolent and keeping everyone safe. Most people didn't know we used MRT, only the elite thinkers knew. And those who knew kept it to themselves for fear of getting hit in the head…

No one could tell me to fuck off. I fancied, "I was the most powerful person alive and also the most important. But I was not rich, and few knew about me.

Then I was in the head of an insolent actress who we'd routinely got into her head and found she was going to tell everyone all about us spies in a tell-all book. It seemed she got her information from a spy who she dated and had sworn her to secrecy. So, I got in her head and had her delete her book and told her to shut up. And she and the spy who had informed her were sent to rehab. I figured we had caught this actress just in the nick of time!

Next, I was involved with a group of gangster hackers who were blackmailing people Online. And stealing bank accounts from various people. These hackers were sophisticated and clever and it was a shame they used their young, bright future to do criminal activities. Anyway, I got into their heads and found them unrepentant and so I duly sent them to rehab.

But many clever people figured there must be a reason that all crimes were solved. Most people thought it was due to our having invisible video cameras that couldn't be detected, everywhere. And the cameras were certainly part of it and had unlimited connection range to our headquarters. And of course, most clever people were watched closely, but with passive MRT, so they didn't know their minds were being read. And we closely watched crazy clever people in particular.

My next case was a clone doctor, who cloned shady characters for a cheap price. It was illegal to clone yourself unless you were a member of the elite. The elite numbered only 10,000 spy personae, but most of them had a few clones and many children. Having children was easy. In the lab, they were fully grown in 1 year with all the memories of their two parents. So, some had children with everyone they came across and had thousands of children. But children cost several million, so basically only the rich could afford it. But people lived on as long as they liked, so many felt no need of offspring. But there were tens of millions of very rich people.

Then I was called in to Europa, Jupiter's Moon. Here was another freak outbreak with some few hundred new freak sea creatures who had been released into the melted ocean and the freaks had eliminated the human colonists who lived there, including the three scientists who'd created them. I came with a contingent of the UW military and identified some of these freaks as basically benevolent, but most hated humans, who had created them. And they didn't like themselves, they said. I didn't know what to do, but finally I installed a rehab facility here. The rehab would help them change their appearance to far more human-like whether they wanted to or not. It was an ugly case, though.

Then I was summoned to Uranus's Moon, Caliban. Here they put-on real-life recreations of Shakespeare and other playwrights, with everyone on the Moon involved in the production, but some actors really died like in the plays. But the people here claimed to be jaded and sad and depressed and suicidal. When I met a few of them I realized that all needed to go to rehab and start afresh. The founders of the colony had been a group of artistic, mad humans who had fled Earth and its "depressing culture." But a lot of tourists came to see the death plays and were disappointed when we put an end to them. But I promised the tourists that the plays would be back only not murder people anymore.

Then I was back on Earth for the Sex Olympics in New York. Many of the best lovers were here. They had events which included stamina, skill and creative sex. But some events featured android love dolls and cerebral loves with holograms. Everyone seemed to be tuning in to watch the Sex Olympics. But I got in the heads of the organizers and accused them of breaking the law with love dolls and love holograms. They said, the people wanted such creatures and they had broken the record for most watched shows. I put a stop to the games and had an assistant announce that love dolls and love holograms were illegal and anyone who loved such creatures would be sent to rehab, like the organizers were. There were protests in the streets defying the law. But we arrested the leaders and the protests fizzled out. And I was angry that our spies in New York were not more vigilant and demoted some of them.

My next case was to determine what had become of stolen art dating back to the mid 20th century. I got into a lot or art dealers heads and of course many engaged in illegal transactions with art which had been stolen over time. I cracked down on illegal possession of art and sent a lot of dealers and collectors to rehab. They tried to tell me the art had been stolen long ago, but I told them they should have returned the art to the rightful owners' descendants.

And then I was sent to Manila, where separatist politicians were trying to violently overthrow the democratic Mayor. I got in their heads and they all mind read that the government was corrupt. And I studied the matter and found that the mayor indeed had enriched himself at state expense and put all his cronies in charge of government companies and they also enriched themselves, but the mayor claimed he had 90% of voters behind him. So, we did a poll and found that just 30% supported him. So, we sent him to rehab in disgrace and many of his followers no longer supported him when they found out about his malfeasance. And we called an election in which we vetted the candidates and so there were only 2 that we were willing to allow. Some of the elite of Philippines, mostly Chinese, said that we were rigging the election. So, we had to get in their heads too and get them to recant and admit they were mistaken. And go to rehab.

My next case was another musician, from Morocco. He played reggae music and was very popular in Africa. But he sang about a united Africa in which he would be the leader. And I studied his profile and found he was domineering and cruel to his lovers, but no one complained. I got in his head and mind read, "What is your vision for Africa?" He mind read, "I will foster the arts and culture and only allow Africans to be the cultural leaders." I mind read, "You are a racist, in this day and age. I am kind of shocked!" He mind read, "I am tired of abuse by white and yellow people and the white South Africans are not welcome. I would seize their assets." I mind read, "I guess you feel you are untouchable with your strong support here in Africa. But no one escapes the long arm of UW justice, and I am charging you with ethnic cleansing, which seems the way you are going." He mind read, "If you take me to court there will be riots." I said, "You will renounce your pan-African plan and stop making music, right now, or I will drive you insane with loud voices in your head." Of course, he tried to fight me, but I turned up the volume until he was unable to function. So finally, he did my bidding. And I didn't even like his music. And I sent him to rehab.

Then I had a meeting with a wayward spy. He said, "We should allow radicals to do their art and science and just keep an eye on them, not force them to stop creating. I spend my time living in the past and enjoy literature, art and music from the 20th century, in particular. Without art, life is boring and without science there is no hope for the future." I told him, "That is nonsense. You have an exciting career and are making a difference for the future." He said, "I am just carrying out your orders as if you were the God Empress of humanity. You are intolerant and stifling the Earth and Space." I said, "Most of our spies have no problem with their duties and enjoy the work." He said, "I want to write a book about a new Bohemia just like in the late 1960's." I said, "I can't allow you to do that. You need to play ball with me!" And a few days later he took his own life. Some of my spies said I had killed him. But I told them the truth, and most could see I was right. After all I had carefully selected the upper echelon of spies to serve me well.

Then I was alerted about a group of scientists on Luna, who had all gone mad and had created mad androids to rule all Luna. These androids wanted humans to partake in hobbies, while they ruled and planned to keep improving android and human intelligence using illicit Supercomputers. There is no limit to intelligence, they said. And it was the time for Superhumans, they said. And they were expecting a visit from me, the Grand Terminator, so I had to sneak into Mars by stealth. Once there I got in their heads, but this set off an alarm and so they hunted for me. But I was using new MRT with invisible receptors at a range of 20 yards which sent invisible MRT missiles to hover over the targets. And so, I finally brought them to heel. And I used UW police to arrest the core of 5 scientists who were involved, and I breathed a sigh of relief as this had been a close call. And of course, these scientists were given a second chance with a visit to rehab.

Then I was off to Mars where a rebel colony was developing weapons of mass destruction. They planned to use the weapons to take over all Mars and beyond. Their leader was quite charismatic, and his scientists were working overtime on weapons such as a virus that spread from computers to people and destroyed everyone and everything in the way. And they were able to clone themselves as android warriors, armed to the teeth. They had already taken a small colony on Mars and were revving up for greater things. I used a number of crack UW troops to suss out their hiding places and soon had gunned down all of them. They made it impossible to take them alive. The people of Mars were so grateful to the UW for helping save them, though my name was not mentioned. I never told the people I was behind the special operations we conducted, leaving the laurels to go to the Generals.

Next, I was called to L.A., where a group of radicals were holed up with advanced weapons, in a hospital, with all the patients and staff held hostage. So, I got in their heads and found they were anarchists and wanted a Spaceship with them on board sent to deep Space and they planned to take some of the hostages with them for safety. But I simply mind forced them to surrender, and all the patients and staff were unharmed. After that everyone praised the brave UW soldiers.

Then I was off to Albuquerque to deal with a real mess Two female spies had killed one another in a dispute over a man. Many around them were crestfallen and confused. Anyway, I said as "Murderers they could not be cloned and would not be eligible for the new experiment with the human soul." And after that I decided to have my spies watch one another more closely. A better system of checks and balances was in order.

Then another potential problem writer, Harry D., this man wrote about madness. And he said, "The Worlds are crazy!" I mind read, "So many people have mental problems (about 65%), that I have trouble handling them all!" He mind read, "About half the crazy people have been driven mad by brain apps as they try to compete in this dog eat dog World." I mind read, "We're trying recently to go slower with brain apps and improving them to suit each individual. And many people go crazy, having no work to do, but I think people are slowly adapting to it and it seems like there are less crazy people than say a few years ago." And Harry mind read, "Some people are good crazy and some are bad crazy." I mind read, "But in general all crazy people are dangerous and have to be watched" And he mind read, "However, I feel for these poor people. Myself, I am a rock of sanity who will never go mad and I hope one day to be President of Europe and help those with mental problems. And we talked about madness late into the night and finally, I mind read, "I like your mind." And I made love with him. And the next day I asked him about his latest book? He mind read, "People these days need challenges. I fancy a World in which everyone challenges one another and dares one another and if one succeeds in the challenge, they will win cash and prizes from the State. I mind read, "We certainly need to help fill up the time for the people, your idea seems to have great merit. And as time rolled on, Harry and I got together a lot to our mutual satisfaction.

Then I had a case with a hell-raiser, Bert T., who was disgruntled with the Tyrant of Australia. He said, "The tyrant had been OK when we elected him but now, he was a most oppressive dictator who cancelled elections and was turning people into slaves and sycophants. I said to him, "The UW doesn't like your dictator also and we will back you with UW troops and you can seize power and reinstate elections. So, it was done. But other tyrants in other places were worried they'd be next, so they joined together in a defensive alliance. This included most of Africa and most of South America and Northern India and Northern China And so, we had to infiltrate the spy networks in these nations, but it was difficult as they were wary. And we used hypnotized suicide bombers to detonate small bombs We promised the suicide bombers that they would be cloned and rich. For their part the tyrants threatened to use nuclear weapons if we didn't leave them alone. So we spies were under pressure from the UW to keep the peace. But we kept using agents provocateurs, to destabilize these regions, and spied on many with MRT.

And then another musician, who made progressive rock albums. He'd been off our radar until recently, when he had a hit with, "Music Pictures." It was a hybrid work with dream visions to go with the advanced music. It replaced live shows for many fans. And many young would-be intellectuals, were much enamored of this band that was called "New Regime." I mind read with him, saying, "I like your music, but you are causing many youth to drop out of advanced schooling and trying to start their own bands." He mind read, "What's wrong with that?" I mind read, "Many musicians are worshipped like Gods, and have fanatical fans. It's too much power." He mind read, "It is magic power and our music brings happiness and fantasy to the people, especially the intellectual elite in our case. And I assure you we in the band are very conscientious about what we are doing!" I couldn't see anything wrong with his approach to life and told him, "I want to love you!" So, we got it on, and I asked him about his next album? He replied, "I am planning to write songs about technology of various kinds. And sing the praises of great scientists, who don't get much fame in this World today and make them into sex symbols. After all they are our best people." I said, "But scientists would not make good politicians and most of them lack charm. And if elected they would bring the Worlds forward with AI, mandatory brain apps etc. which is undesirable. But we spies have to watch them carefully as they are still powerful, and some scientific research continues like greater speed in Space and genetic DNA therapy. You know, you cannot make such an album." He asked, "But who is watching you personally?" I replied, "We spies have many checks and balances and watch one another carefully." Anyway, he was another good lover for me and I was glad to make his acquaintance. In hindsight I don't know why. I shouldn't have loved him.

Then another less difficult case in which a woman was giving deadly new diseases to unsuspecting lovers. I mind read with her, "What do you think you are doing?" She mind read, "I hate men. If women ruled, life would be good and worth living. As it is it is dog eat dog and everyone has become uncharitable." I mind read, "But there are plenty of women rulers today." She mind read, "But they are brainwashed to compete with men. And Armageddon is near." I mind read, "You have an attitude problem and have become a cruel woman. So, I am sending you to rehab." And she went kicking and screaming.

Then there was famous movie director who had a knack for finding lucrative scripts. Everyone knew him, but he had bought out a few studios and was now going to make some highbrow films. He mind read to me, "There's not enough really clever movies out there." I mind read to him, "What did you have in mind?" He mind read, "I'd like to make a movie about clever female spies and the cases they take up. And also, I'd like to make a movie about a man who was born with nothing who becomes a zillionaire; it would be a feel-good movie for thinking people. Also, I plan to make a film about two lovers, a man and a woman who go just the two of them, to Star Sirius, a journey of two years and drive each other completely crazy, which just goes to show you monogamy is dead." I mind read, "Best to avoid that one about the spies; we like to operate in secret and don't want our methods and philosophy broadcast to everyone. As for your other films, don't make them too deep. Keep things light-hearted." He mind read, "That's the stupidest thing I ever heard! Clever people need clever movies. And I don't care what you think." I mind read, "I'm just thinking you have to be careful what you do!" And he mind read, "What do you spies want? A World of morons?" So, I could see I wasn't getting anywhere with him, so I simply said, "I'm watching you, and I am in your head! And I hypnotized him."

My next case was a doozie. Fred F. had been a well-vetted general who suddenly snapped and stole a nuclear weapon. And no one knew where he was. Finally, we picked him up on satellite video and were able to follow him to his hide out. UW police surrounded the house, but he answered his phone and said if we broke into the house, he'd detonate the bomb. I was in his head but was afraid to yell lest he set the bomb off. So I employed a seldom-used tactic of killing him instantly with MRT. We told the UW police he'd had a heart attack. Case closed and we kept it out of the press, so few knew about it.

Then there was the case of the missing President of North Brazil Federation. The Vice President stepped up to take power and declared the "President had been kidnapped." So I got in to some heads and found it was a palace coup and the cabinet members were all in on it. They felt the President was a phony and they couldn't stand the obsequious State he had created. I knew that the President was a pompous fool, and we would all be well-rid of him so I didn't look any further into the case. The body was never found.

My next case involved a scientist who had created a genius android, which was unlawful. And he used experimental teleportation to send the android to Betelgeuse Star System. But most of us spies were afraid to teleport. But finally, one high ranking spy agreed to go armed with a laser. And he went to the same planet as the android, who was alerted by the appearance of our spy. And he came to investigate but was gunned down by our man who was then teleported back. We all congratulated him on a job well done and we promoted him higher. As for the scientist who had created this Frankenstein, he was sent to rehab, needless to say.

Then it was the case of the woman who claimed to be the most imaginative person alive. She had sold her daydreams for zillions, putting her in the top 200 richest personae category. I wasn't familiar with her work, so I mind read to her, "What are you working on now?" She mind read, "I just had a dream in which everyone was crazy and had trouble functioning and went about shouting and screaming and grabbing one another and devouring one another." And another recent dream, a nightmare too, she mind read was about, "A World of feuds, vengeance and tyranny and the people all hated one another and tried to kill one another." I mind read, "I can see how your nightmares are popular." And I let her go as she seemed relatively harmless. And I had her hypnotized for the second time in her life.

Then I took time out to write the story of my life for the benefit of my closest assistants. I described how my father was a famous architect and my mother was a rich entrepreneur and at age 5 (fully grown at birth), I went to Berkeley to learn more where I met my first true love. He and I spent countless hours talking about the state of the World. And then one day, I was selected by local spies to join them, and I never looked back, and I wrote to my assistants about my deeds in the cases I had so far described and did the same with ones that follow. And I told them when I was in school, I never imagined telepathy was so important. And I was quite surprised about the spies' philosophy. And I had done a lot of good work as a spy, but there were plenty of tyrants and dangerous people to keep me busy for the foreseeable future. Most spies supported me unequivocally, but some pointed out that the fact that there were still tyrants in the World, showed that I was all too fallible. And some criticized me for not doing more.

But then it was back to business, and I was in a conversation with another would-be writer. This one was from North India, Ahmed K. He wanted to write about the future of MRT. But he didn't know us spies were really utilizing it. Instead, he envisioned a World of love in which everyone would be honest with one another and there would be peace and goodwill. I mind read to him, "If everyone used MRT, the whole World would be topsy turvy and the people would be insane. To have no privacy is certainly an anathema and MRT would allow for strong minds to control and denigrate the less clever. And the rich would dominate the poor. And the ruthless would rule." He mind read, "We'll make new laws, so that people can't be abused and no getting in peoples' heads without their permission. And most mind reading will be passive rather than active. But if you drove people insane you would be designated for rehab." I mind read, "We are already experimenting with MRT among different types of groups. But we are taking a go-slow approach and change peoples' minds gradually." He mind read, "I'm writing about the far future, though." I mind read, "To write about the far future is relatively harmless. But know that I am watching you!" He said, "I would never write anything dangerous!" But I hypnotized him anyway.

Next, I was dealing with the leadership of the North American Federation, where they wanted to make all drugs legal. This included experimental drugs for virtual sex as well as drugs to make your mind work at 100% and drugs to enhance MRT and drugs to make one crazy for material possessions. Also new panacea drugs which led to euphoria, yet total functioning. Also new brain apps. And neo-heroin which was less addictive than normal heroin. And so on. I told them, "Making experimental drugs legal and available would be a tragic mistake." They told me all drugs can be good. And they didn't want to throw dealers and users in jail. The less people incarcerated, the better. I said, "If you must make such drugs available, they should only be given out by doctors and the doctors should closely monitor the effects of the drugs and share the data with others. Perhaps we could make it a good thing. But the drugs to enhance MRT must be forbidden, and so too drugs for virtual sex.

Then I had a meeting with the Worlds' Union of service workers. The Union was concerned about jobs being replaced by robots. I told them, "We at the UW are working to preserve as many jobs as we can. But in tyrannies in particular abolished most service jobs, saying, no need for such jobs and the robots made them a lot of money to spend on pet projects." The Union asked me to do something about the tyrants, I said, "In all probability tyrants will be with us for the foreseeable future." But I vowed to myself we would get rid of all tyrants.

So, we stepped up our agents provocateurs in tyrannical States in Earth and Space. And we infiltrated the spy services carefully and made pacts with spies in those States. We told these spies if they started a revolution, the UW would move in and send troops. But many such nations had nuclear weapons, so it was very dangerous. Ten years ago, Northern China had used nukes on Southern China. And tens of millions were killed.

And we sent troops to support recent revolutions in Asia and so now the World was 77% democratic in terms of population. The UW was pro-democracy but there were still some tyrants in the UW. But most elected people and tyrants worked as spies for the UW before they took control. Most of the elected leaders were UW spies.

My next case was with another would-be writer. He mind read "I want to write a book about different peoples' sexual fantasies. It will be a documentary about the rich elites' fantasies." I mind read "The true elite are the top 10,000 spies." And I mind read, "What is your fantasy?" He mind read, "I dream of a genius woman who will dominate and control me and make me her slave." I mind read, "It sounds like an interesting project, it seems harmless." He mind read, "It's a world of sex!"

Then I was dealing with another young writer who wrote a book about the future being dominated by a single tyrant who forced everyone to have sex with love dolls exclusively so as to make them more attached to the State. And he gave all the people panacea drugs to keep them happy. And he would use MRT to control the people. I mind read to him, "Why write a Dystopia?" He mind read, "If we are going to avoid problems in the future, we need to talk about them now!" I mind read, "Go easy on writing about MRT as it is very powerful and in the hands of tyrants and radicals, it is very dangerous." And I planned to keep an eye on him, and hypnotized him.

And of course, tyrants of the modern World were mostly not UW spies, but we were in all of their heads So finally, we started getting into the heads of wayward Nation rulers and Mayors with new long-range

MRT and took many by surprize. Basically, we rendered them catatonic, and there were some coups, mostly of better people than the tyrant including our representatives who wanted democracy. We started revolts in all major dictatorships. I considered these events to be my finest hours. And made the future look bright and took away the specter of Armageddon. Henceforth there would be no tyrants and only our democratically elected spies would be in power.

So, I allowed myself to celebrate and threw a wild party and invited all the top 1,000 spies. The party went on for a week and I loved some of the men for the first time. I now controlled all leaders…

PART FIVE: 2152 SPRING/SUMMER

But then it was back to work, and I had to deal with a fraudster who had swindled people he didn't like out of trillions and had given the money to charity. I didn't know how to deal with him, but finally I mind read, "You can't take the law into your own hands and do as you please. So regretfully I am sending you to rehab. He mind read, "But I was doing a lot of good!" I mind read, "Us spies will take care of the goodwill acts. We are changing the World as we speak and will deal with all the bad personae."

And that gave me an idea to tax heavily people who the spies didn't think were good. The tax would also come with notice that if they didn't change their ways they'd be sent to rehab. And I hired millions more spies so that we could watch everyone. I was of the view that everyone was potentially dangerous. Some people we watched complained that we were Big Brother and said that their privacy was being violated and their right to free speech and freedom in general had been taken away from them.

And some said that now that the threat of Armageddon had been taken away, there was no need for spies to watch everyone. But I felt I had the momentum and wanted to take as much power as I could in order to bring about a glittering Utopia.

So next, I had to deal with a woman who was undeniably sexy who had slept with a number of bigwigs including Presidents and other leaders and she wanted to write about all their secrets that they had told her by way of pillow talk. I worried she would talk about us spies so I got in her head and mind read, "What do you know about us spies?" She said, "I am shocked you are in my head. I only know that spies are watching everyone and I won't write about MRT, I promise." I said if you do I'll send you to rehab. She said, "I know enough about rehab to fear it greatly." So, I had her hypnotized.

And then I was mind reading with a famous video game player. He mind read, "Video games are improving and are ever more popular and champions like me are widely feted. I am a sex symbol, unbelievably." I mind read, "How do you feel about mind-controlled video games in which the best minds win out every time?" He mind read, "I don't know if I am the most clever, but I have a pretty strong imagination. And I imagine mind-controlled games would be a whole new kind of games. Maybe such games are the future but would probably be dangerous to one's sanity." I mind read, "How are you handling the fame?" He mind read, "Is that what this is about?" I mind read, "Partly." He mind read, "You must be referring to my proclivity for having orgies with illicit drugs with fans. I assure you we are under control and pose no threat to anyone. I mind read, "But some of your fans say you used mind control psychedelics on them and caused them to do crazy things." He said, "People who do crazy things are crazy and have many excuses. That drug doesn't change peoples' mindsets. Many of my followers are fervent and mad." I said, "I suggest you remove yourself from future competitions or you will end up in rehab." He pleaded with me to leave him be. But I told him, "It was an ultimatum, actually." And I had him hypnotized, he resisted the hypnosis but we threatened to kill him if he resisted. And so it was done.

Then I was mind reading with a man who purportedly had his mind altered to be a Superhuman by scientists working for the Government of Northern India, contrary to UW law. So I passively listened to his thoughts for a few days and concluded he was among the smartest people alive, but he didn't seem to be any cleverer than me. Still, I mind read to him, "How do I know you are a Superhuman?" He mind read, "Of course at first look I appear much like any other clever individual. But I imagine a World in which everyone mind reads and the more advanced tutor the others to have them catch up intellectually." I mind read, "I don't think it would work. He said, "Also I envision people are born with bigger heads with better brains from the get go. That might work even better. And also DNA changing drugs which will improve imagination. And of course new, improved brain apps. We shouldn't hesitate to improve the human race anyway we can!" I mind read, "You're just a dreamer, but you are good. However know that UW spies will be watching you." And as for the scientists who had created him, we watched them very closely, also. And we hypnotized him just to be sure.

But in this new World, spying and intelligence were the exclusive right of the UW only. So we didn't need permission from the local government to watch anyone we pleased. In some countries, some people were against us spies but we rearranged their thinking.

Then I was mind reading with the leader of Southern Brazil. He was a spy but apparently thought he was above the law. And he had his scientists develop the perfect servant. These servants were human and sexy but were obsequious and slavish. And many people wanted to have such a servant. Our local spies failed to discover what was going on there. So I had to come in and wipe up the mess. My first action was to get in the heads of these servile creatures and send them to rehab. Then I went after the scientists and asked them why they had broken the law? They all said, good service workers are hard to find, and servants were better than robots. This was a common modern-day phenomenon, trying to create AI; the technology was there. And so I had this knowledge erased from the databases and it wasn't taught in school. Anyway, I told these scientists no human should be a slave and I am sending you all to rehab. But one of them got a message out to the press that spies were mind reading and forcing people to back down from their dreams. And the press broke the story but then pulled the story as we controlled the big wigs at the Worlds' news companies. In their retraction, the press said it was a case of the boy who called wolf. I told my spies to keep a closer eye on scientists everywhere and if they had any problems to call me.

And then I was mind reading with a clone of Marilyn Monroe. I mind read with her, "How does it feel to be a sex symbol?" She mind read, "All men seem to like me and feel they want to be part of history. Modern women are far different now than in Monroe's time. Women are aggressive and righteous and not so kind." I mind read, "Women today are tough, and we live in tough times." She mind read, "I don't see why women can't be more kind and nice and feminine. And why are you in my mind?" I mind read, "As a key sex symbol you have a lot of power, and you want to change women. And you've said men are too greedy and selfish and easily dazzled. It seems like you want to change the World and Space. But men and women have been carefully cultivated by us spies through education and MRT and we instill in them a sense of justice and responsibility and gregariousness. And those who have mental problems are encouraged to seek therapy. It's a pretty good World and Space scenario. We wouldn't want you to rock the boat." She mind read, "But the fact that so many have mental issues indicates that society is far from perfect. I think you should help me to improve society. Many people will listen to me." I said, "I'm impressed by your vision. So, we will use you as a spy to watch powerful men and see how you do!" She said, "You give me a sense of purpose. I won't disappoint you." And we set her up with the World's richest and cleverest men and she was able to watch many men at one time. And no one suspected she was a spy.

Then I was mind reading with, Boris G. He was Russian and always drunk on vodka. But he had invented virtual reality Super chess with a larger, oval board with five players and 9 superimposed fields of battle and 36 pieces for each side, including some pieces which had new types of movements like jumping over pieces and pawns that could take out other pieces straight ahead in addition to the side, and some that could go backwards, and four queens. But also, the game gave one the ability to capture pieces and hold them hostage so that one could buy them to set them free and so one could get rich playing. And people bet on the elite games and the winner collected part of the bet. I mind read to Boris, "You've invented a splendid game that brings entertainment to others. And I would like to offer you a position as spy for the UW. Many highly clever people play your Super chess and I want you to watch them and make sure they don't harbor radical thoughts." He mind read, "Actually there is a lot of camaraderie amongst chess players and I know some people you'd consider dangerous." I wished him good luck and I helped promote his game.

Next, I was mind reading with a young woman who claimed to have loved 10,000 men, about 5-6 a day over the course of several years. I mind read to her, "I hear you only love clever men." She mind read, "Only the cream of the crop." I mind read, "I'd like to offer you a position as a spy. You can get your lovers drunk and get them to tell you their secrets." She mind read, "Yes I know a lot of secrets and some men I have loved are despicable creatures. And with many it's a love-hate relationship." I said, "You can report directly to one of my close assistants."

Then I met a woman who was ugly in my opinion. I mind read, "Why don't you get plastic surgery and genetic therapy to improve your appearance?" She mind read, "You'd be surprized how some drunk men go for me. Some even think I am beautiful." And I mind read, "We are working on making everyone beautiful and give everyone eternal youth. And I am signing you up for genetic therapy, you'll be glad after you get it and will thank me." She mind read, "I guess I have no choice." It was a small case, but the lesser spies didn't know what to do with her.

Then I had to confront another writer Betty G. who had written, but not published, 3 novels. The first was about how the leaders of the Worlds claimed that we lived in Utopia, but most people were not happy and were crazy and were insatiably greedy for material possessions. The second novel was about a new Utopia in which everyone was naked and everything they said was monitored by an infallible lie detector and they lived in the jungle, and the jungle had no mosquitoes. It was a primordial Paradise, only better and everyone had eternal youth of course. The third novel was about me and talked about how I had sent many radical geniuses for rehab and didn't tolerate any dissenting voices. And she wrote I had ruined the World for everyone. I mind read to her, "You are so bold and yet so foolish. How did you ever think you would get away with that third novel of yours?" She mind read, "I see now what I suspected all along that you were using MRT to force people to do your bidding." I mind read, "We live in dangerous times, MRT is necessary." She mind read, "It is all just a stunt by UW spies to take total control; talk about totalitarian!" I mind read, "People like you are so egotistical, you are blind to the greater good and the good of the elite. And you want followers who worship and adore you. You are the anti-Christ." She mind read, "I suppose you are going to alter my mind for daring to question you?" I mind read, "You strike me as suicidal." She mind read, "Rather I am a desperado who is like a rat in a cage. I mind read, "Rehab is not so bad. You'll feel better afterwards." She mind read, "I don't want to be the slavish mind that you demand of everyone." So of course I sent her to rehab. And destroyed all copies of her books. And forgot about her.

Then I was dealing with one of the big wig movie producers. He had recently made a film about Armageddon and how there were few survivors who were miserable. So, I mind read with him, "Now that we have all governments being democracies, the chance of nuclear or biological holocaust is far less than before. He mind read, "Humans these days are not of sound mind, and all it takes is for one dictator to seize power and conscript everyone to fight. And there are many scientists who would be willing to develop dangerous weapons in exchange for elite treatment." I mind read, "Don't worry us spies are watching everyone and are right in their heads. So there will be no surprizes. Peace is virtually guaranteed." He said, "But in this World of rapid change, our fate could change on a dime." I said, "Your latest movie disturbs the public and makes people think that such a fate could come true. Please don't make any more disturbing films." And I let him go, after hypnotizing him.

Next, I was mind reading with a man who many thought was a true saint. He had done a lot of charitable work with those who were relatively poor and made sure many got a good education and got governments to give the poor more money in exchange for their vote. I met him and mind read, "Your work with the poor is noble, but what do you think about those who want all the poor to improve their minds?" He mind read, "I've never mind read with anyone before and I am afraid. But I think there is enough intelligence in the World already, we don't need more." I mind read, "But there are many mind-altering drugs, some of them permanently and other treatments. And many people offer jobs to those who have enhanced their minds." He mind read, "It is developing into a rat race for all. But the elite only care about themselves. And we need more champions of the poor and lonely and depressed. No one should fall through the cracks." I mind read, "But the powers that be mostly care about the downtrodden but the only ones to survive beyond a few years are those who have enhanced their minds. The downtrodden are going extinct and their suicide rate is very high." He mind read, "I think your impression of the modern day scenario is cruel and though it may be reality, it is not the Utopia that everyone seems to want." I mind read, "Charity can only go so far. People have to stand on their own with their own philosophy." He mind read, "I say the common man should be celebrated not oppressed. There is room for all on Earth and in Space." I mind read, "There's no grandeur to be common and ordinary. People have to take their best characteristics and build upon them." Anyway, I let him go and continue his work, though I thought he was barking up the wrong tree. I have to admit, I don't know everything.

And next up on my busy schedule was a woman who claimed to be the most beautiful woman in all the Worlds. I looked at her and thought this woman is a real knock out. She wore clothes of light that were semi-transparent and showed off her beautiful body. She mind read, "There are billions of men who want to love me, but I try to love those who seem to be the brightest and nicest." I mind read, "You know you have a lot of power as one of the most beautiful women. And how will you use that power?" She mind read, "More and more women are virtually copying my face with minor alterations and there is also the new Superhuman beauties. I don't feel I can compete." I mind read, "Don't worry most men are sentimental for the past and want to love someone familiar. New beauties are generally thought of as cold-hearted and decadent." She mind read, "It tell you I am still the best lover in the Worlds, but it won't last. I plan to take up art in my retirement." I mind read, "I would hope we are building Worlds of beauty. But sometimes beauty clashes with intelligence. And not all beauties look intelligent. It is all in the eye of the beholder, as they say. But although I am a female, I think you are the most beauteous of people." She mind read, "I at first thought that you were in my head to drive me insane, but now I realize you are a good woman, who wants the best for women everywhere." I mind read, "That's a nice compliment. And I wish you the best of luck in your exciting future." I didn't need to speak with her, but I did just to be sure.

Then I was talking with the World's fourth richest personae, a woman named Cleopatra B. She had gotten rich in building domes of all sorts. Like under Earth's seas and under the now melted seas of Europa, Triton and others. And in cold cities on Earth. And even invisible anti-missile domes. She had a monopoly on domes. And she also made a lot of money on electric air car charging stations. Her patented stations were somewhat quicker than others and to some people their time was extremely valuable. I mind read to her, "What are you doing with all your zillions?" She mind read, I am speculating on real estate in the Centauri Tri-Star System. I own most of the best planet's real estate there." I mind read, "The governments of Earth are ending deep Space colonization. And we are bringing the colonists back. Haven't you heard?" She mind read "I had heard rumors, but can't believe Space exploration is being curtailed." I mind read to her, "Do you contribute to any charities?" She mind read, "I pay a lot of tax and its the government's prerogative to look after those with mental illness." I mind read, "What about your politics? She mind read, "I support the Progressive party. I want all out progress." I mind read, "But many are left behind in the mad scramble to enhance our lives progressively." She mind read, "In my opinion, people try and go too fast to improve their minds. They need not hurry. It's no sin to be less intelligent than others. Just as long as they improve slowly but surely. One day, I figure, everyone will catch up and there's a limit to human intelligence." And I mind read to her, "You pass the MRT test, but I will keep watching you once in a while." She mind read, "Why do you need to mind read with me in the first place?" I mind read, "Because you have a lot of power, and you are therefore potentially dangerous." And I had her hypnotized.

And I then was mind reading with Debbie S. She was a General in the UW army and she kind of shook things up by insisting all UW soldiers be armed to the teeth and be able to wipe out scores of the opposing forces. But some such soldiers had suddenly snapped and killed many. I mind read with the General, "Why are you making soldiers so powerful and why can't you determine which soldiers are dangerous?" She mind read, "We need help from you spies to vet potential soldiers. And as for arming soldiers with powerful weapons we can reduce the numbers of military personnel. And strike fear in the hearts of our enemies." I mind read, "Of course we can help you vet the soldiers more than we already do. In my opinion, every soldier should be clever and all troops should be considered officers." She mind read, "Too many cooks…" I mind read, "Most troops would be lieutenants and captains, but the number of Generals would still be 1,000." Debbie mind read, "At present our troop strength is 300,000. I think it could be trimmed a bit with cleverer, more powerful soldiers in the field." I mind read, "Now that all nations were a democracy, the need for soldiers is less." Debbie mind read, "You spies should be commended for your good work." I mind read, "We prefer to be a mysterious secret!"

Next up on my busy schedule was a man who was accused of selling drinks in his bar that had drugs in them which permanently altered the brains of the customers, who said they didn't recognize themselves after drinking in his bar, but felt inclined to keep coming here. I mind read, "What do you think you are doing?" He mind read, "I didn't think I'd get caught. But I was just trying to improve the minds of my customers and keep them coming back. It was a packed crowd every night and many told me they felt great at my bar!" I mind read, "You are seriously in breach of UW law and must go to rehab." I didn't waste time with law breakers, generally speaking.

And next I was mind reading with an idiot savant, Troy L. He had proved that Jupiter could become a sun with bombardment by special catalysts. But he was dressed poorly and lived in relative poverty and had no lover. I pitied him so I made love with him and gave him a few million dollars. And bought him some fashionable clothes of light and I introduced him to one of our spies who wanted to love him. But so far Jupiter had not been disturbed and there were colonies on Jupiter's Moons that were vulnerable. I mind read with him, "What is your next project?" He mind read, "I want to create the perfect human female lover. Such a woman will be a designer baby who through trial and error will be a great lover. I am inspired by you." I mind read, "I am glad you are inspired. I guess everyone will want designer babies who will be perfect lovers. In my opinion there isn't enough sex in the World today and as long as your designer babies are fully human, I don't have a problem with them." It all fit in with my dream for Utopia everywhere. And I even experimented off and on with making the perfect male lover and the love was good. I continued with it when I had free time. And if I ever decided to retire (which I probably wouldn't), I'd take up such a hobby

I then was mind reading with another writer, who was similar to Troy (above). He was half-way through a novel about perfect humans. People would be ambitious but not greedy and would be very clever and very kind and all would have many lovers and would use MRT to love one another and there would be no crime due to MRT. I mind read to him, "Actually it sounds like a good future, and I will consider giving MRT to everyone, but it will take a lot of time for planning and execution."

And I made sweet love with him and encouraged him to write more about the future. He mind read, "I'd like to design Worlds in which everyone is involved in making deep movies. Entertainment will be important in the future as people will have a lot of free time. And it will give people something to do." And I mind read, "What do you think about AI making films?" He mind read, "I'm sure you spies won't allow it!" I mind read, "Then carry on with your good writing. It was nice meeting you." But I had him hypnotized for the second time.

And the next persona I mind read with was Charles C., an owner of a lot of social media companies. Many people worked and socialized on social media, and no one worked in offices. And everyone had lots of connections with people they liked or had business dealings with. It was all virtual and some wanted to make love with the images in 3-D. A total mind fuck. But we spies figured the images were like holograms and it wasn't the same as real sex, so we didn't allow it. People, like Charles, pressured us to allow virtual sex. I mind read with him, "No way will we allow it." He mind read, "It's the 22nd century and we live for progress." I mind read with him, "If you insist on virtual love, we'll send you to rehab. We have to keep this World for the humans and not 3-D freaks." And I mind read, "We spies are thinking of limiting virtual work and correspondence, if not eliminate such things altogether." He mind read, "You want us to go back to the atavistic past. Yet you claim to be progressive." I mind read, "We know what is best. We spies are the best." He mind read, "I know you also tell a lot of writers and scientists that they can't practice their craft. You are holding back progress and tell one another you are the best and that those who don't agree with you are dubbed radical fools and you threaten everyone with rehab. It is tyranny unlike anything we have seen before." I mind read, "I am letting you go because I believe you to be an honest, good-hearted person, if somewhat misguided. Just don't try and do anything crazy." And I had him hypnotized.

Then I was mind reading with the creator of the human soul. I mind read, "We really didn't need a soul after death. He said, "Many wish to go to Heaven when they die as a reward for their hard work. I mind read, "But your Heaven is for disembodied spirits whose only pleasure is thinking thoughts. Most people who go to Heaven are disappointed. And we spies have decided to ban all souls and eliminate those who already exist." He mind read, "You are on the road to hell, yourself." I mind read, "I enjoy my position as Head of spies and will never die!" He mind read, "You are a dirty rotten killer." I mind read, "If you don't disassemble Heaven, we'll have you executed and we are sending you to rehab." And I figured getting rid of souls was a real step forward...

I then was talking with a woman, Jeanette R., who mind read, "I have invented a number of new spices and new stem cell meats that are all very popular. Many say I am the best cook in all the Worlds." I mind read, "Yes, I concur. But with new anti-fat pills many people eat all day. Like pigs." She mind read, "It can't be helped. It is better than having androids who don't eat." I mind read, "I suppose." And she cooked me up a storm, I'd never eaten so much. She mind read, "Life is all about pleasure!" I mind read, "We're all looking to get our kicks."

Next, I was mind reading with an ex-con who had set up a gang of thugs who robbed people on the street. But we had their DNA, so were able to hunt them down and assign them to rehab. The leader mind read with me, "You are far too powerful!" I mind read, "You should've been more astute and should've known not to commit crimes." He mind read, "What of you and your thought crimes!?" So, I had him committed.

My next challenge was a woman who broke a lot of hearts and many of the people she broke the hearts of were powerful men, some of whom complained to my office about this woman. I took one look at her and figured her beauty was unparalleled. I mind read to her, "Why do you break so many hearts?" She mind read, "It's a dog eat dog World, and a woman has to be tough to survive." I mind read, but you've ruined the minds of a number of fine people." She mind read, "Such men are weak and are of no consequence." I mind read, "You are cruel and reckless, and I am sending you to rehab to correct your severe attitude problem."

PART SIX: 2152/2153 FALL/WINTER

Then I was confronted by a writer of mysteries, Amber R. She wrote about killing high profile people, and I didn't like how she portrayed the killers as very clever and, in some cases, justified. I mind read, "You have caused a number of copycat killers to murder important people." She mind read, "Such killers would have committed murder anyway without reading my books." I said, "But you glorify murder, and I am pulling your books and sending you to rehab. You should've known better." She mind read, "But I am famous and loved by many." I mind read, "You are reckless and heedless of the pain you've caused." I personally thought her punishment was somewhat draconian, but I was under pressure from other spies and people who'd been murdered.

Next up was another irresponsible writer, Liz W. She was a science fiction writer. She had written a number of Dystopias. Her latest was about a World controlled by ruthless spies who stifled creativity and forced everyone to be mediocre. And if people said, they were unhappy, they'd be sent to rehab. I mind read to her, "Where did you get your inspiration?" She said, "A few of my lovers were spies." I mind read, "How did you think you would get away with such a diatribe against the powers that be?" She mind read, "It's good for people to know what the future will be like." I mind read, "People don't want to know the future. And the cleverest, best people all work as spies. Our Worlds are in good hands." She mind read, "If you are stifling dissent and creativity then you are not the best. It is a rule of people who are not geniuses." I mind read, "But surely you realize that without the spies, these Worlds would have gone through Armageddon. We have brought peace and prosperity to the Worlds. It is truly Utopia." She mind read, "You're Utopia is shallow and boring and is almost evil. There are no deep books to read nor deep movies. And music is nearly all shallow pop. And science hasn't come up with much recently. You supress everything good." I mind read, "You seek power and fame. You are power-crazed and heedless of what damage you are doing. You don't have any original ideas, you just borrowed from your spy lovers. You are just a hell-raiser, and I am sending you to rehab." This episode left a bitter taste in my mouth. I had to admit although we'd basically created Utopia, it wasn't the best for everyone. Perfection was elusive, but we were trying our best.

Then I met with a musical duo. Two female songwriters, Annette and Ashley. They were pop musicians, but many people liked their jingles and melodies. They had millions of fans. I mind read to the two of them at the same time, "Do you consider yourselves to be wise? Annette mind read, "We've met a lot of important people and have a pretty good idea of what humans are like." Ashley mind read, "We are on the road to being the most popular band in the World! We had to be wise to pull that off. Success eludes the vast majority of musicians!" I mind read to both of them, "What are you doing with your fame?" Ashley mind read, "We donate billions to mental health research. I have 2 brothers who are insane." Annette added, still mind reading, "We also set up a music school for precocious students. Many of our graduates are famous pop musicians." I mind read, "If you were leaders what would you do?" Ashley said, "I'd slow down progress and help the common people be mentally stable." Annette said, "I would make it into a World of music in which famous musicians were in positions of power and people would all have a guitar to play music and sing all their conversations." I had considered these two to be spy leaders, but they were too radical, so I bid them adieu and moved on. And had them both re-hypnotized.

And then I was communicating with a pair of twins, who were co-chairpersons, of a love company. They were Stacy and Audrey. Their company was for the elite people, and they provided great male lovers for an expensive price. Their lovers were well-trained by the two of them; they were both former high-class escorts. I mind read, the two of them at once, "Don't you feel we live in a society of love and kindness?"

Stacy mind read, "All our gigolos are very clever and make great conversations. Some say our gigolos are the best in the World." Audrey said, "I think our lovers are geniuses." I mind read, "So what are you doing with the money you make?" Stacy mind read, "We use the money to expand the company and try to attract artistic genius males to work for us. Some of our gigolos, figure this is the best job available. And it helps pay for their artistic endeavors." Audrey mind read, "We live in an era in which women are fully liberated sexually and know what they want. And we figure we are providing a valuable service, and we are saving many artists from relative poverty and contributing to their success. I mind read, "I want to try one of your best gigolos!" So, I did, "And he was a struggling painter, Will. He mind read, "I'd like to paint future beautiful women." I paid him double and wished him well. And I mind read, "You can use my face as a starter for one of your masterpieces." He said, "This mind reading is really something. I'd like to paint how energy emanates from your head and improve your nose a little!"

So next, I went to a plastic surgeon to improve my nose and she and I both agreed it was an improvement. I figured I had one of the cleverest faces in all the Worlds. And considered myself to be a great lover.

Then I was summoned to Ganymede to the freak colony there. They were all multi-sexual, which meant they had new sex organs, like bumps and mucous membranes and had multiple sets of lips and many of them had strange green faces that had only one eye in the center of their forehead. But I was able to mind read with them in English. I mind read to their leader, "What's wrong with human bodies and minds?" She/he mind read, "What's wrong with a little variety?" I mind read, "But you acknowledge that you are a branch of humanity?" She/he mind read, "We are just like a group of clever human artists. And we insist we have a right to live and hope humans will like our work." So, she/he showed me some of she/he's work. They were pictures of she/

he in the future with amazing futuristic architecture. And she/he showed me his/her movie which was a love story about how she/he loved an androgynous human, but it was ultimately unrequited love. Life is sad was the message of this film. And she/he wanted to love me but I mind read, "My mind is open, but freaks don't turn me on." He/she mind read, "You should try and open your mind a little more." And I kind of felt sorry for these freaks. But I had to send them all to rehab. And their population here was 1,000. Most of them had been created in this year. I was earnestly trying to stem the tide of freaks. But as they said, they were people too. And these freak people seemed to pose no threat, but their very existence was contrary to UW law. And many people criticized me for shutting down the freaks. And I got some death threats, but these were easily traced, and their proponents sent to rehab.

Then I was dealing with a man, Bob B. who was obsessed with me. He kept sending me e-mails and 3-D holographic images of himself. In the e-mails he wrote stories about him and I and our life together. Finally, I confronted him, and he mind read, "I am overjoyed to make your acquaintance. I feel you are the most important persona in the World today. And will you love me just once and then I'll cease to bother you." He was quite handsome and obviously had some plastic surgery, and I loved him for one night only. The next day my assistants all criticized me, but I told them I had to get it out of my system. And true to his word, this obsessive man, left me alone. And I was quite flattered by the whole thing.

On a more serious note, I was mind-reading with a woman who was a famous movie star but now wanted to make serious films, i.e., deep films. And she made one about a far-off World in which there were only 2 survivors, a man and a woman. And they tried to prove that monogamy was still possible. But finally, a relief ship came and with it 100 settlers. And they remained friends, but admitted they were sick and tired of one another. And loved other people. So, the jury was still out on whether pure monogamy was possible. I mind read to her, "There are many who tried but failed to be monogamous. She mind read, "I think, with the right kind of people, anything can work." And I mind read to her, "What about her upcoming films?" She mind read, "I am thinking of making a future film about how people will change the color of their skin to various colors and will spend all their time at parties. But they will sleep 8 h a night for their mental health (many modern people took drugs so that they never slept) and will take anti-hangover pills. Masquerades would be the most popular, but there were many themed parties and some parties required acting skill, but these people were all actors and actresses and sold their party videos to other Worlds." I said, "I am sure your films will do well." I had my doubts about her getting into "deep films," but clearly there wasn't anything to worry about with her movies. However I had one of my lesser spies keep an eye on her, and had her re-hypnotized.

My next interview was with a woman, Margo, who started a fan club for me. There were tens of thousands in the group, but they didn't know really know me or know my work. They only understood that I was Chief Spy, which I wished they didn't know. And some of them composed cartoons about me fighting evil and discord. They all wanted to meet me and begged for an audience with me. I told them, "To quiet down about me, I was just another woman trying to do her job." Anyway I set them on the path to bothering people I didn't like. That kept them busy. There were many Mayors I didn't like, but they mostly weren't dangerous.

My next mind reading session was with an African musician, Tok, who played like Jimi Hendrix and had a lot of followers after his first album. The album was called "A Synthesis of Discord and Accord." The lyrics were about how the World could be improved if he was Emperor. There were songs about a World ruled by artists with him as leader. And they would have a lot of music, and everyone would have skill at least with one instrument. And they would have a lot of parties and good times. And there was a song about how no one should fall through the cracks of modern-day society. And another about how the Space effort should be greatly enhanced as there was plenty of real estate out there and plenty of pioneering opportunity. And another song was about how future spies would read minds and dominate Earth and Space. I didn't like that particular song, obviously and confronted him about it. He mind read, "I am willing to be a spy too. My music is the perfect cover. No one would ever suspect I was a spy." I mind read, "If you are going to say that I have plenty of work for you to do under the cover of your musical tours!" And he and I became lovers and I toured for a while with the band getting in the heads of various leaders.

I had now gotten in the heads of hundreds of local Mayors. Anyone who was a clever Mayor was watched by my assistants and me. And we watched clever politicians who had bad tendencies as Mayor, too. Every year we were in more heads. I estimated we'd been in 4 billion heads out of a population of 10 billion, so 40%. And we watched anyone over 17 who showed intelligence or madness. And we had a great number of universities to teach people to be spies.

Next up was a man who was a famous TV personality. These days TV was all in 3-D, and everyone knew this guy, named Terry O. He asked me, "How can I help?" I mind read, "Amongst your fans, identify those who are against the established order!" He mind read, "Many of my fans wear their heart on their sleeves and some want me to change the Worlds. I'd be happy to help!" And Terry hosted, "Eerie Nights" that were basically about mass murderers and talked about how these murderers thought. And many potential murderers wrote to him and asked him, who they should kill. It turned out to be a great trap and we caught a lot of would-be criminals through his e-mail. We found them guilty of thought crimes.

Then I sat down with my top assistant, Laura T., and mind read to her, "Do we really need to arrest people for thought crimes? I mean I thought about killing many people and of course wasn't punished." She mind read, "Of course we arrest them when they start to plan an attack of some kind, and usually they do misdemeanors first and we get in their heads and watch them. It is necessary to send would-be hardened criminals to Rehab." I mind read, "But couldn't we just send spies to befriend them and give them good advice and discourage them from crime and encourage them to have fun instead? Sometimes would-be criminals just need a good lover to keep them in line. We can send escorts/ gigolos to them for free." Laura mind read, "To do that we'll need more spies. But yes, we could certainly be kinder now that the tyrants are on the way out, and the future looks bright."

So, then I was mind chatting with a woman who was designated for rehab, but had appealed her case to my office. She, Mimi, was going to rehab because she had stolen all her ex's money when they broke up after being monogamous for 6 years; 6 years was almost unheard of. In her defense, she mind read, "My ex physically and mentally abused me." I mind read, "Why did you stay with him for so long then?" She mind read, "He said he would kill me if I left him and I have him on tape threatening me." I mind read, "Any sane woman would have left such a lover if he threatened you at all. Maybe you liked the abuse! Anyway, you are guilty of theft and going to rehab. And I remonstrated with my assistants for referring such an easy case to me. But they told me she was a miserable woman and they felt sorry for her. I told them, "Maybe sometimes we spies are too kind!

And then I was dealing with a mad woman who claimed she was the craziest person alive. She mind read, "I dared the President of the North American Federation to accept my ideas for change. For example, I want only the craziest people to rule this crazy World and want everyone to admit we are all insane. Humans today are out of control greedy and selfish and don't love anyone but themselves. And people are going to Space in droves for no good reason and it's draining the treasuries to send colonists to Space. And freaks are everywhere and are a big disgrace. I tell you it is madness, and I am loving it in a sick kind of way." I mind read, "Those who are too crazy are sent to rehab and come out of there sane. I won't arrest any mad persona unless they are violent, but we watch the craziest. Some are capable of anything, good or bad. But you are definitely not the craziest persona, you seem rather to be upset about the Worlds. Now you just need to change your frustration into political action." She mind read, "I am capable of anything and frighten myself. Maybe I could voluntarily go to rehab. I mind read, "I am sure you will feel better if you do." And so she did.

My next case was with another writer. This one was named, Pye. He wrote about how he'd met a number of geniuses, but none of them seemed inclined to do science or the arts. He suggested that the spies were preventing geniuses to realize their potential. I mind read, "Why do you think so?" He mind read, "Some of the geniuses he'd met had given me hints. And now you are in my head to prove it." I mind read, "You'd have been wise to keep such ideas to yourself. But oh no, you had to disturb shit that no one wants to hear about." He said, "What about free speech and freedom to have privacy?" I mind read, "We allowed free speech in the past, but it only led to problems. With the advent of democracies, spying on intelligent people picked up and it is spies that have, in the modern World brought peace and nearly everyone wants that. And we all have to pay the price for peace. We can't have radicals like you rocking the boat. And you are going to rehab." He mind read, "You people have no conscience. You've made a dull World which basically kills interesting people." But I paid no attention to him. And I tracked down the people who had tipped him off. It was no game, we spies were very serious.

Then it was a mad scientist who had lived in the Underground for years. The Underground was supposed to be a place of freedom and attracted all sorts of clever people. But now we had infiltrated the Underground with MRT to get into their heads. This particular scientist had developed MRT himself and used it to control people of the Underground. I mind read to him, "MRT is for spies only and we can't tolerate an Underground of radicals who are all opposed to the powers that be. I am sending everyone in the Underground to rehab. He mind read, "Fuck you!" And I thought to myself what an insolent bastard, quite beyond the pale. There turned out to be 67 radicals here. I figured my underlings had been doing MRT on the group for some time and now they were all caught up in the MRT trap. There seemed to be hope for a few of them, however. Like one woman who was a polymath and did good art and didn't seem to be a radical. And another woman who had just drifted into the Underground and was quite sane. Radicals were an anathema to me, but if they weren't radicals, they generally weren't a problem. We taught people in university that radicalism was an anathema. And all radicals did was rock the boat in the pursuit of fame and fortune. I figured all radicals had an attitude problem and were ungrateful for the wonderful World we had created.

Then another musician. She was Anne and played popular music with a lot of horns, kind of like the Big Bands of the 20th century. Her music was purely instrumental, but she had millions and millions of fans, and so she had power. I mind read to her, "What do you think of the future?" She mind read, "I thought most famous musicians were sell outs, but now I realize you were in their heads forcing them to stop making good music." I mind read, "If you were President of Europe, what would you do?" She mind read, "I know you are trying to entrap me and get myself to confess to radical ideas. But if I was President, I would have people have more children and to live for a happy future and not let the spies take over. And Bohemians would rule. But I guess that's not what you want me to think. Will I be punished?" I mind read, "As long as you keep your ideas to yourself, there will be no problem. Make as many instrumental albums as you like, it doesn't matter." She mind read, "You shouldn't be charging people with thought crimes and sending them to rehab." I mind read, "Consider this a warning." And I hypnotized her. I was tired of musicians and their power. Maybe one day we could ban music as well as science fiction literature. Personally, I didn't like music, nor did I like to read about Dystopias.

Then I met a man who claimed he was a Superman and was a model for future people; many women wanted to have children with him. I mind read, "How do I know you are a Superhuman?" He mind read, "I have great mathematical ability and have discovered some new habitable Planets in Space. And I have a theory that matter and anti-matter are the same thing, and nothingness is the same as something." I mind read, "That's a preposterous theory. I don't think you are anything special." And he mind read, "I am going to run for election on a platform of making it a government of technocrats, scientific geniuses to rule the Worlds. And to bring back AI Supercomputers with Super genius capabilities to help improve humanity's children. AI would allow us to all have no tedious work to do only inspirational work. Of course, some people are easy to inspire." I mind read, "Making scientists political is an anathema and a government of technocrats would be in all probability mean that the elite would rule and those with no scientific ability would be left behind." He mind read, "Everyone would live in an amazing future of science and will be turned on to science. Those with poor scientific ability could still be lab assistants and anyway all the youth would be scientifically gifted thanks to Supercomputer engineering." I mind read, "Stop you are driving me insane!" He mind read, "It's the future that most people would want and you are not broad-minded enough to be able to envision it!" I mind read, "Just because you are very clever, doesn't mean you can take control. You would only ruin the World and force people to futilely be cleverer and cleverer with untested minds." He mind read, "You fear intelligence, that's your problem." I mind read, "I am backed by the most powerful minds in all creation. But we don't allow radicals to take control and what you call Superhuman is just another radical philosophy. And I am sending you to rehab." He mind read, "You are a coward." But off he went to Rehab kicking and screaming. It was another disturbing experience for me.

And then I was watching a woman who wrote fantasy dream-like books. For instance, she dreamed of Worlds of clever fantasy creatures. A world that entertained and amused humans. I mind read with her about, "Creating creatures that are too clever and non-human is an anathema to all good people. Please keep it to literature, don't like, try to actually make such fantasy creatures, if you must write. It would be far better if you just wrote about human fantasies." She mind read, "Who are you to tell me what to do?" I mind read, "I am in your head, and I am in charge of your ultimate fate. Surely you can see that!" She mind read, "Fuck you!" I wasn't surprized she would say that. Lesser spies said they couldn't do anything with her. So, I told her, "You are going to rehab. Have a nice life." And she went away quietly with my guards.

Next, I was talking to one of the Worlds' richest women Daphne. She was a lesbian and wanted to create a colony on Mars, just for gays, clever gays. So, she came to me for advice. I mind read to her, "Just make sure the people in your colony don't try and make themselves cleverer. It's OK to be bored some of the time. No need to improve and create Super gays." She mind read, "But gays need to survive in the future, so I think they should all have gay children." I mind read, "That's fair enough, but I don't think you should ban straight people from your new colony." She mind read, "But I think gays are by nature more open-minded than others and so are superior. I don't want them to be tainted by straight people. We will have our own scientists and artists and don't need to open up to others." I mind read, "OK, we'll only send gay spies to watch over your colony." She mind read, "Why is it necessary to watch us and get in our minds?" I mind read, "In the dangerous future all clever people need to be watched. Surely you can understand that." She mind read, "I guess I have no choice." So, the colony was quickly set up and many people who were bisexual wanted to try it out. And many freaks applied, but were not accepted. Some on other colonies thought this colony was just another freak show, but they excelled at the arts. For example, they attracted the gay writer, Heinrich, who wrote about a future in which everyone had a maximum open mind, and everyone was gay. On the colony, Heinrich opened a university for opening minds in the first days of the colony. Another, Drew, a painter painted rainbow people in a rainbow landscape and painted everyone who came to the colony. And there was a musician who made pop music and was the most famous musician in the Worlds. The initial population was 1,000 but it grew exponentially. The leader of the colony, Daphne proclaimed, "All gays should come here." I said, "Whatever turns your crank. But don't bring radicals to your colony." Daphne said, "For sure I won't!"

Then I was talking to a scientist, Dennis, who said, He could identify DNA of most radicals, so he helped me set up designer babies everywhere without radical DNA. I figured it would save me a lot of work. And bring peace to these tortured Worlds. I gave this scientist a zillion dollars and he also helped me with automatic MRT that would probe everyone and identify radicals. I didn't mind a little automation; after all we had Automatic Production Machines which produced all the food and goods. Just as long as the machines didn't think, they were OK.

Then I was faced with a vigilante who murdered criminals who were released from rehab. He admitted he'd killed 40 over the space of a week. He'd been planning the murders for some time. I mind read to him, "Once people were released from rehab, they posed no danger to society." He mind read, "They are getting off too easy. I think we should bring back capital punishment." I mind read, "You should have known better than to murder these people. So now, you are going to rehab." And relatives of the people he murdered demanded that the murdered ones were cloned. And so, their wish was granted, but the clones were based on the rehab changed versions. Rehab altered DNA.

PART SEVEN: 2153 SPRING/SUMMER

Next up was a man who had altered his own DNA to make himself cleverer. Of course, it was highly experimental, and he was totally crazed. His mind was just a jumble of crazed phrases, and he was almost catatonic. I got through to him though that he needed to go to Rehab where I figured they could fix him. And he went along gracefully and humbly.

Then I was dealing with a writer who had been called the "Hemingway of our times." He was the most popular writer. I checked in on his mind and mind read, "What do you envision for the future? He mind read, "The future will look after itself. We need to focus on modern times. Why are you in my head?" I mind read, "You have a lot of dedicated followers. And are therefore one of the most powerful people of our time. How would you like to change the World?" He mind read, "I'd like to see a more loving World, can you achieve that?" I mind read, "We're working on it, but we don't want to see people fall blindly in love with writers. Writers who are successful like you have millions of potential lovers." He mind read, "But it is hard for me to find soul mates. I believe most people these days are cold-hearted and unhappy." I mind read, "Well, do what you think you can make the World a little warmer." He mind read, "I think so; in fact I'll make it my mission to do so." And I had him re-hypnotized, just to be safe.

And then there was Cherry. She was a famous woman who sold patented perfumes and colognes. Some said her scents drove them mad with desire. She also sold make-up that made any woman more beautiful. I mind read to her, "What is the future of body and face care?" She mind read, "People will use unique DNA stimulating scents tailored to one's own DNA or that of your lover. And make up will be replaced with uniquely beautiful plastic surgeon's face. People will work with the plastic surgeon to pick a face they are proud of." I mind read, "You do good work, but please make your products available to everyone; within their price range. Everyone deserves to be sexy." She mind read, "Anyway expensive cosmetics are no better than cheap ones; just as long as no one steals my patents!" I mind read, "The UW is dedicated to enforcing patent law, even in deepest Space." She mind read, "There's no limit now for how good cosmetics can be and I am excited about the future."

Then I met a woman who claimed to be the best farmer in the Worlds. She'd introduced hardy plants to Mercury, Venus, Mars and the Moon and was thinking of expanding deeper into the Solar System. She was thought to be the best biochemist in Space. She mind read, "Now the Moon appears green from Earth so everyone could see progress being made in Space." I mind read, "And your plants have helped terraform Space, helping to create a better atmosphere." She mind read, "I want to grow Super trees of gigantic size to really change Space environments." I mind read, "Everything you do is good, you got my vote for woman of the year." She mind read, "I didn't seek fame in my work thus far, I just want to improve Space for all." I mind read, "What do you do for an encore?" She mind read, "I want people to come to Space and be scientific pioneers and further the cause of science. I would use Supercomputers, but I know they are banned." I mind read, "Yes, there is no reason to use Supercomputers." But terraforming is noble." And I had one of my spies keep an eye on her, and hypnotized her.

Next, I was introduced to the President of The Northern Mercury Alliance. He had a nickname, "The Golden Sun King." And the people here lived under domes that let some UV radiation in so, that everyone had dark skin. And they had a lot of solar power here and so could make gold out of lesser elements in the metallic surface. And they could simply mine gold. The price of gold continued to rise, now it was $100,000 an ounce. The people of Northern Mercury were all rich and had the best social services anywhere. Many wanted to come here, but they only allowed in people who truly loved gold to a mad degree. Their clothes were gold foil, and their air cars were gold plated and so too their apartment blocks. And they sent pioneers to other Solar System Planets and Moons, searching for gold, but Mercury was really the place of gold. And there were a lot of other metals here which could be changed to Gold using abundant solar power. I mind read to the President, "There's more to life than gold, for sure." He mind read, "Gold was something that never disappointed, in this World of disappointments." And that's how it was here!

Next, I was mind reading with a woman who claimed to have 300 World Records. Most of her records had to do with survival all alone in Space. She mind read, "She didn't mind being alone as long as she had plenty of entertainment. And I am semi-famous for my World Records. I desire to be famous!" I mind read, "It's a lonely set of Worlds for sure and many who are socialites are themselves lonely. But there are certainly worse things than loneliness. She mind read, "Most people are boring anyway; I am glad to try mind-reading with you!" I mind read, I sense there is something you want to tell me, but are trying to block." She mind read, "It's just that I am looking for someone to believe in and haven't found anyone yet. But maybe you are that person." I said, "Your future is bright. I'll keep you updated on World developments from my censored perspective." And I had my spies keep an eye on her, and re-hypnotized her.

And next up was another man who claimed he was the cleverest writer ever. He'd written a book about android potential. Such androids would be able to survive in empty Space. And androids could be designed to not have human instincts like greed and the desire to breed and egotism. And would be pure creatures of intelligence. He mind read, "At least we should experiment with them and not ban them altogether." I mind read, "Human instincts are what makes humans great, and we should make sure that humans live on into the future. And remain in control. There's no point in replacing ourselves with different creatures!" He mind read, "It's evolution and it's destiny. A new branch of the species homo. And humans are improving, though they are all crazy, nevertheless they are wiser and have better imaginations and some places only accept new immigrants who score high on IQ tests. And most designer babies are designed to be cleverer than their parents." And I mind read, "As long as they remain recognizably and functional like humans, it is fine. But surely, we don't want to replace ourselves with freaks or machines. We are definitely not machines, like androids, and are a natural product of evolution" He mind read, "I just think we should try and design our successors with an open mind." I mind read, "There's such a thing as a mind that is too open. The prize for intelligence doesn't go to the most open-minded!" He mind read, "You disturb me!" I mind read, "You will not put your book up for sale and will stop writing science fiction. And I'm going to keep an eye on you, to make sure you don't get involved with the wrong people. Consider this to be a warning." And I had him hypnotized for good measure.

The next case was Michael T., he was a tutor at a university. He tried to make students be all they could be. To find out what skills they had and build upon those. I mind read, "You are known for making something out of everyone." He mind read, "Everyone is born a potential genius." I mind read, "I'd like to clone you many times over and have lots of children. We need more people like you!" He mind read, "Yes, that's a good idea, I thought of it previously but lacked cash. My salary is relatively humble. And clones cost $100,000,000." I mind read, The UW will pay for 100 clones and 600 children for you." And he mind read, "I could set up a dozen universities with them and the children will be born as adults with all my memories and those of my favorite female personae and most of the children will be groomed to be tutors. And the clones will all be tutors." I mind read, "Exactly!" And he mind read, "The courses will of course be 100% on line, so there will be large classes, but I will get to know each of my students and give them some personal advice And everyone could apply to come to my universities, and those who can prove they are imaginative will be selected. So my schools will be for the rich elite. I feel I can really make a difference." I mind read, "What about the lesser minds?" He mind read, "If you give me still more money I can open schools for the common human!" I mind read, "Consider it done." And among elite circles we quickly had more imaginative geniuses. But many of them wanted to write books, and I wanted them to just enjoy life. There were all sorts of new writers, most were mainstream and good and popular. But there were also many radicals. I told Michael to discourage radicals from writing, and report all radicals to my office.

For instance, a graduate from the school was a fledgling writer, Patrick who said that radicals on the lunatic fringe should rule the Worlds. He mind read, "It would be a good mix of different ideas." I mind read, "The problem with radicals is they don't care who gets hurt and typically don't work as part of a group. And they disturb a lot of shit. Radicals are an anathema. He mind read, "Give me a chance." I mind read, "I know you have just been born, but we are sending you to rehab."

Another writer had been an air car salesperson until she went to Michael's school. Now she was writing a novel in which everyone in the future was cowardly and sold their souls for money. The human race had become a race of wimps and spineless people. And she mind read, "It serves as a cautionary tale. And I mind read, "Let the spies look after the future and stop upsetting everyone." She mind read, "But there are so many possibilities for the future. We need to have everyone thinking and debating the future." I mind read, "It's better if the cleverest decide the future and we spies are the cleverest." She mind read, "I've read books of the past and think I am right up there in terms of intelligence." I mind read that, "The spies have kept the World together for centuries and trust me we are the cleverest. Writers are just clever idiots." She mind read, "MRT is too powerful. It gives spies near total control and spies aren't elected. You have usurped control and I am sure that vast majority of people wouldn't support your MRT program especially now as we live in peace in the Worlds." I mind read, "But spies are the one's who engineered the peace and we don't want any more tyrants, so we watch everyone." She mind read, "Watching the ruthless and cruel is one thing, but interfering with the best intellectuals is an anathema. You have overreached your power." I mind read, "The World doesn't need more Dystopias and I am forbidding you from writing and if you don't stop, you'll be sent to rehab." And I had her hypnotized.

And then there was a writer who had been a lowly security guard until he came to Michael's school. Now he wanted to write about an Emperor of the future. The Emperor, would unite all the States in Earth and Space. And he would use his spies to supress dissent. The spies were very well paid and underwent MRT testing to ensure that they were loyal. I mind read to him, "We spies don't want to have one person only in power. In fact, we are supporting new City States and decentralizing power. And we have plenty of spies in each State to keep the peace. It is Utopia." He mind read, "But spies are ambitious and many would like an excuse to seize power. Sooner or later an Emperor will appear." I mind read, "But we spies watch one another carefully and though I am high ranking, many of the lesser spies are in my head too." He mind read, "Well you've allowed me to read your mind so, I guess it's true. Maybe I'll write about something else!" I mind read, "I am watching you." And I was glad he didn't realize the Emperor already existed; it was me.

And I was getting tired of dealing with writers spawned by Michael's university. So I left dozens and dozens of cases to my underlings and moved on to other cases.

So next I was dealing with a woman, Guinevere, who had the most famous air car amongst the many Worlds. The air car could go to Space and so was really a Space car and the car's exterior and interior design was unparalleled. But it was patented so no one else had such a nice air car. I mind read with her, "How do you feel about some people today being completely mobile and living in their air cars?" She mind read, "I think it's an excellent thing, just like our hunter-gatherer groups. But why are you in my head?" I mind read, "I am just checking in with you. Us spies, we watch everyone. She mind read, "You get in everyone's head? It seems like too much power." I mind read, "We live in volatile, dangerous times. Spies are necessary to keep the peace." And I mind read, "By the way how do you feel about the future?" She mind read, "Are you trying to entrap me?" I mind read, "We want to survey everyone for their thoughts on the future." So, she mind read, "I feel that progress will continue in the way its going now as the same people, i.e. you guys will be in charge. More Space colonization, more democracy, mediocre art, science will probably be capped, and the common people will be cleverer. Something like that." I mind read, "You know we spies are very adaptable, but the future does seem to be predictable. And that's a good thing."

Then I was mind reading with a woman who was Ms. Mars. I mind read to her, "What is the future of Mars?" She mind read, "We will continue to terraform the Planet which will take some new scientific pioneering discoveries. And the population will continue to grow exponentially and will attract many young scientists who are full of promise. Rather than AI, the future of science will be in terraforming Planets and Moons and faster speeds. The scientists will have to work within such constraints. Your leaders who you support have made it clear that AI is not on the table for future development. I have been told by Martian spies all about it." It was a problem for us, loose-lipped spies, but on the other hand people got the message. And I mind read, "Describe your perfect lover!" She mind read, "I've loved so many, I hardly know where to start. Basically, though I find I go for spies as they can tell me the future and are basically the cleverest. I mind read, "I think it's kind of a romantic thing to date spies. I myself have dated many spies, but also many others. I think I have an open mind." She mind read, "Do you really?" I mind read, "I can accept anyone who is working for the greater good, and who is not radical or self-serving." She mind read, "These days there are lots of perverts and selfish people, but not so many radicals; you've prevented radicals from happening. Maybe you can focus on selfish people and freaks now." I said, "The freaks are a disgrace, but don't really bother me, and we fix them anyway with rehab. As for selfish people, we try to educate everyone to be selfless, but we have a long way to go before we reach this goal. But I envision a future of congenial, happy people." She mind read, "What about the huge number of insane people? Recent polls indicate 65% are having mental issues. And many won't admit it. You are creating a civilization of mad people." I mind read, "We spend countless zillions on mental health and rehabilitation. In my humble opinion we should stop encouraging dumb people to improve their brain. Only the best should seek to use brain apps. And maybe we should give the common people true love and happiness and a job to do. But though I am a high-ranking spy I can't control totally other spies who want the status quo. But spies as a rule, only care about the intelligentsia." Ms. Mars mind read, "Is there indeed anyone in control? I mind read, "Just let us say it's difficult to control all the varying spies." She mind read, "I have heard rumors that you are in control!" I mind read, "I will only say I'm one of the most important spies." She mind read, "If so, why are you mind reading with me?" I mind read, "You have a lot of influence and power here on Mars!" She mind read, "I'm very flattered to be sure." And I had her hypnotized.

And then I was mind reading with the Mayor of Philadelphia City State. She was affiliated with our spies, but was one of the few independent Mayors. I mind read, "Is it the city of brotherly love or is it the Flyers of the 1970s?" She mind read, "It is a free city, freer than most and I am not overly influenced by the spies." I mind read, "But don't you think that freedom is overrated? She mind read, "I know that you spies have arrested some of our citizens and altered their brains, but you have the weight of the UW behind you and so there's nothing I can do about it. But I still feel that I personally am free to act as I wish. Unless you have a problem with that?" I mind read, "I just want to know what you think of the future?" She mind read, "It looks like the

Armageddon scare is behind us. That's a big achievement of you spies, I think. But the future seems bright for humanity provided you aren't a radical." I mind read, "So you know about us?" She mind read, "It's a shame, many of the radicals whose brain you altered are like kittens compared to the lions they once were." I mind read, "But surely you understand the danger poised by radical thinkers?" She mind read, "Now that you have all countries now democracies, I think you should let up a bit on the radicals. In my opinion most great science was done by people who thought outside of the box, radicals in other words." I mind read, "There's a difference between thinking and radical thinking. Good science is just good thinking, but revolutionaries and radicals have no use in the modern World." She mind read, "Really?" And I felt she was kind of a radical, but I let her go and told her to, "Carry on with your work!" But I had her hypnotized.

For my next mind conversation, I chose the Mayor of Triton, Neptune's Moon. She was known for her "tough rule." I mind read, "I think you are doing a great job here on Triton!" She mind read, "So then you know that I send all radical people to Rehab." I mind read, "Yes and your scientists have done great work with the oceans of Triton." She mind read, "But many of the spies don't like the fact that we have so many Earth fauna in our oceans." I mind read, "Such wildlife is harmless; just be sure there are no freaks among them! The colony you've created here is chock full of scientists and I would like to take a tour of your oceans." She mind read, "Let it be!" So, I went down in a submarine and saw amazing sea creatures. She mind read, "Most of the scientists wanted to give these sea creatures hands and the ability to communicate with MRT, but we have been warned by the spies not to do so. Anyway, we are proud of our oceans!" And I wondered where this would evolve to in the end. She mind read to me, "And our sea creatures mostly live on neo plankton and are peaceful." The oceans had a thin ice cover but were heated by nuclear reactors. I mind read, "Do they have intellectuals, these creatures?" She mind read, "It is an egalitarian World in which all were considered equal. However, at the moment the 50,000 human colonists are the only ones with the vote. But the elite here have several votes each." I said, "As long as they are free and content, I guess it's fine." She mind read, "I foresee a World which is a refuge for those who don't belong elsewhere." I mind read, "No, you will do no such thing. We don't want to create a hotbed of discontent." She mind read, "As you wish. But I am disappointed." I mind read, "Better to be disappointed, than to be sent to rehab. So, I had her hypnotized.

I then was interviewing a woman who was a paranoid schizophrenic. She mind read, "You are in my head, why?" I mind read, "We haven't been actively in your head. You have paranoid schizophrenia, It's a common disease. We can cure it with a trip to rehab." She mind read, "It's all you, I know it is!" I mind read, "Why would we be in your head?" She mind read, "I'd formed a league of MRT victims and I myself am a writer. I wrote about the spies using MRT to control everyone." I mind read, "Why would you be so reckless?" She mind read, "As far as I know, we still have free speech everywhere these days?!" I mind read, I am sending you to rehab where you'll be free to talk about anything you want." She mind read, "I think you are evil." I said, "Fuck you!

And next up was a woman, Tamara, who was a hell-raiser. She'd organized a protest in Mexico City with thousands of air cars blocking the mayor's home. The protest was against the price of energy. The protestors believed the power companies were making record profits and the common people couldn't buy enough energy. The protest quickly spread to other cities around the Worlds. I mind read to her, "It's a temporary problem, we'll have prices down within a week. The cause was sabotage of some nuclear reactors, and we captured the saboteurs." But I mind read to her, "Your protest sets a dangerous precedent. You should have known we'd fix the problem We live in a virtual Utopia, and you are still not content. So, I am sending you to rehab. Your hell-raising days are over." She mind read, "Now I understand why the World is so fucked up."

Next I was talking to a Mennonite farmer, Stephen. His orthodox, atavistic group still thrived. I didn't want to upset him, so I just talked with him. I said, "I've heard many city people are flocking to join you." He said, "Many people are disillusioned with modern society, but we have plenty of wholesome work for them to do on the farms. It is my understanding that everyone is going insane in the modern World. Perhaps one day everyone will join us." I said, "There's no way that people will give up their material possessions and won't want to leave enlightened society behind. And few want to do hard physical labor. People today work with their minds." He said, "Well for those who are not satisfied with the glitter of modern civilization, we'll be here!" So, I tried to live on such a farm for a week. It was exhausting work and there was no man who wanted to have sex with me and there were no drugs allowed here, nor alcohol. But I was so tired, I just slept and worked but I felt awful and was sick from the real meat. And I told Stephen, "It was certainly not for me." He said, "Well thanks for trying it!"

My next case was a newborn in an adult body. He mind read, "I am having trouble getting used to my memories, which are of course of both my father and mother." I mind read, "That's par for the course. You'll get used to it. He mind read, "I think many who have both female and male memories become bisexual." I mind read, "That may be but it doesn't matter. We are producing well-balanced fresh young minds." He mind read, "I want to change into an androgynous human." I mind read, "You are not the only one. One in a thousand of the populace is androgynous. But he mind read, "I will be a crusader for androgynous conversion for all humans." I mind read, "We spies desire the vast majority have a fully human body with just one sex only, we don't want you to campaign against that." He mind read, "I am sure that androgynous humans are the future." I mind read, "Not on my watch." And I had him hypnotized.

And then, I was mind reading with a woman who had invented long distance MRT with tiny needle receptors shot in the heads of people which can communicate with satellites so we could reach people anywhere in the Solar System. I mind read, "That's quite the invention! We can certainly use the technology." She mind read, "But I worry the invention will make spies too powerful. And I would like everyone to read one another's brain. A technology for the people." I mind read, "I don't think people are ready for that. As it is we get passively into most minds we watch, we generally only use active MRT when there's a problem, and it is very dangerous to do so. People would drive one another completely insane if everyone had access to mind reading technology." She mind read, "MRT needs to be upgraded so that one can block out personal thoughts; secrets." Anyway, the new technology improved our operations outside Earth, in particular and the UW rewarded her with a zillion dollars for the invention. I mind read to her, "What will you do with the money?" She mind read, "I have many pet projects to work on. Like robot builders who can copy one another and build up a domed deep Space colony all by themselves. And building a more powerful telescope at the edges of the Solar System. And creating super foods which help improve one's brain. And so on. So, I took no action here, other than having her re-hypnotized. Of course, as a rule once people were hypnotized, we had nothing to worry about from them. However, it was good to re-hypnotize people some times.

My next case was one of the wealthiest Solar System traders. He brought water to some Planets and Moons and metals to others. And those who were clever as well as those who were cloned traveled with his ships. He now had 156 ships and planned another 100 this year. He was fabulously rich and looked like he would get a whole lot richer. And he said he would live forever and eventually own everything. I mind read with him, "What is the future of Space?" He mind read, "Faster speeds will lead to colonization of deep Space and my ships will carry DNA like sperm and egg banks and astronauts who will be pioneers with small robots that can build large ones and so on." I mind read,

"What about gold?" He mind read, "The price of gold will rise and eventually it will pay to transport it long distances." I mind read, "What role do you think the UW will play in colonizing Space?" He mind read, "So far the UW police have brought peace to Space. No Star Wars! And I think that is excellent. And everyone will be free, no slaves, nor wage slaves. I pay my crews a handsome wage and we have had a few accidents, but people can buy Space insurance; for example if they die, they will be cloned." And I mind read, "How's your love life?" He mind read, "I have 100's of wives; they are everywhere and I always travel with several of them." And I wished him luck in his business. And I had him re-hypnotized.

And then I was confronted with a woman, Joan, who had set up a colony on Luna for women only. It attracted many lesbians, but also women who wanted a break from love and romance. Being a woman, I was welcomed here. I found they had great hairstyles and clothes and shoes and hats. And everything was pink. And I mind read with her, "What is the future of women?" She mind read, "I think most politicians will be women, who are kinder and nicer than men and have better EQ! And women want peace." And I mind read, "What kind of art do you promote here?" She mind read, "We have a lot of poets and artists and musicians here, all of whom are ardent feminists." And I wished her good luck with her colony. But I figured feminists were no longer needed. And had her hypnotized.

My next case was with a man who was a self-professed hippie, Cedric. He mind read, "I am all about peace and love and sex and drugs and classic 1970's rock and have set up a hippie commune here on Mars." I mind read, "What about modern music?" He mind read, "We all know that you spies have persecuted modern musicians who played advanced music." I mind read, "Let's just say that we've had some misunderstandings with some popular musicians." He mind read, "We have cloned many 1970's stars, but you spies have sent many of them to rehab. I hate you people." I mind read, "But we allow your colony to exist and if your musicians don't have a big ego and aren't too greedy and power-crazed, we get along with them most of the time." Cedric mind read, "I think you spies are jealous of great musicians." I mind read, "Some are like the pied piper and lead people astray." And I told Cedric, "Well we'll be watching you." And he cursed us spies. And I had him re-hypnotized.

Then I was dealing with a gambler who had bankrupted a colony on Luna. Many thought he had cheated at the card games and then cheated at Russian roulette to gain all the colony's capital. I looked into it and sure enough he had cheated. So, I forced him in his head to give back what he had embezzled and pay for clones of those 12 who had died playing Russian roulette with him. I mind read, "You know you've got to go to rehab?" He mind read, "I was playing with a bunch of cheaters, I just won because I outfoxed them. It is a vicious game, modern gambling." I mind read, "You are leaving Space and going into rehab in NYC, you won't see me again."

The next case was a woman, Leanne, who was accused of using subliminal advertising. Mostly sexual images and music with hidden messages. She mind read to me, "Painters use subliminal images all the time, and receive no punishment. Why are you after me?" I mind read, "Most painters are using subliminal images as art. But you are using them just for profit. You are out of control greedy and need to cease using subliminal images or you are going to be in rehab. She mind read, "But you get deep into the heads of people, and rearrange them which is far worse than simply trying to sell good products." I said, "Good luck in your new life." And I had her hypnotized.

Then I was mind reading with a potter/sculptor, Martina, who wanted to sculpt some of our spies. I mind read with her, "The whole idea of spies is to be secret. We don't want people to know what we are doing." She mind read, "But you are the true rulers of all the Worlds in which humankind is found." I mind read, "OK you can make a full museum with interactive cloned minds of us spies, but only spies, the good elite will be able to go to the museum. It will be part of our Spy University in NYC." Martina mind read, "I've never heard of it." I mind read, "It is a secret." She mind read, "It's hard to know reality if one isn't a spy. It's a secret World. And I'd like to be a spy!" I mind read, "Increase your social contacts with artists of all kinds. And I'll give you my vid-card." She mind read, "But I want to know your secrets!" I mind read, "Just know that we don't tolerate radicals. That's who you should be looking for."

For my next case, I had Mira, a woman who was the former Ms. Galaxian. She mind read, "Our modern era is one of unparalleled beauty. I myself have had genetic therapy to enhance my face and body and this DNA will be passed on to my children when I have them. I mind read, "Yes, genetic therapy made everyone sexy, but you are one of the most beautiful woman I have ever seen. No wonder so many important men want a piece of you." And she mind read, "I'm thinking of having some clones in order to deal with the backlog. Almost every lover I had was great." And I mind read, "What is the future of beauty?" She mind read, "In time, beauty will change step by step until peoples' faces and bodies would be unrecognizable to us in contemporary times. Beauty will go through some fashion cycles. But it takes guts to have a really different face." I mind read, "I want genetic therapy, too!" She mind read, "I have inspired many people to get genetic therapy. And I am quite proud of that. "I mind read, "It's going the way of beauty being taken for granted and so people can move on to other characteristics to search for in a love." She mind read, "One day she'd like to tailor beauty to the individual beholder." I mind read, "Yes, just let science catch up! You are a true inspiration!" And I had my spies keep an eye on her. And hypnotized her.

Then I had an altercation with the fiery politician, Blue Fire. She mind read to me to, "Most politicians these days lack passion. They are all like zombies." I mind read, "I think it is good that politicians are calm and cool." Blue Fire mind read to me, "Did you have something to do with it? Am I in danger?" I mind read, "You say, you want to have neo lie detector tests on all politicians. It is quite an upheaval." She mind read, "Don't you think it is perfect? Or do you think MRT is better?" I mind read, "Lie detectors could be very useful to us spies. Why don't you set up lie detectors in as many states as you can? A truthful society would be a good one." But she mind read, "Why didn't you do it before?" I mind read, "We are currently increasing the number of people we watch and lie detectors will help us, but sometimes people who speak what they believe is the truth but are mistaken. MRT is for the problem radicals. You are one of the good citizens, you have nothing to worry about with us!" She mind read, "What a relief!"

So, we figured the time was right for neo lie detectors. We simply asked people if they had any radical thoughts and got straight to the heart of the matter. So lesser spies could do it, no need of MRT. We were now watching everyone and had spies infiltrate all organizations and large groups of friends.

My next case, was Benjie. She had invented MRT designed art, by which you put on canvas what was in your mind and your unconscious mind while you slept, as well. She did it under our supervision, and we spies, all agreed that it enabled everyone to do good art. Of course, we had nothing to fear from paintings, so we released the technology to the Unions of Artists. They had to apply for MRT to be used only for painting, it was not configured for communication. I mind read with Benjie, "Now we will live in a World of art!" She mind read, "I'm kind of surprized you allowed MRT art, but I am glad you did!" And I figured painting was a good outlet for creative minds and many who came out of rehab took up painting now. We actively promoted it for everyone. And some artist colonies popped up, with approved musicians and approved writers joining in. We kept a close eye on such colonies, of course.

Then it was Harvey. He had formerly gone to rehab and when he came out, he went to a remote location in Northern Canada and lived as a hermit. He had formerly been the leader of the Worlds' writer's union. And he had had a wicked mind. I checked up on him and he was now anti-social and did no artistic work of any kind. He mind read, "I'm just surviving." I kind of felt sorry for him and I had sex with him, and mind read, "You should move back into a city and be part of life again." He mind read, "I hate modern life!"

On a lighter note, I met with one of my favorite lovers, Mark O. He was a high-ranking spy. And this time he opined, "I don't know how we could make this World any better. Nor make the future any brighter." I told him, "Yes we have made a true Utopia." And this time I loved him for a month, and we traveled to some exotic places and met some interesting spies in those places. Like in Paris we met Louie who was saying, "Some people these days are so proud and haughty. We need to improve education." I told him, "We'll make you education minister for the North American Federation and see what you can do!" And another we met was Tammy L. in Germany She was saying, "I wanted to be President of Europe." I said, "You can run in the next election, and we will assign people to your campaign." And another spy we met in Serbia, "Wanted a challenging position." So, I sent him to an undersea colony where our spies were at each other's throats. It was quite rare for our spies not to get along. But, it was definitely a challenge, meeting so many people.

All in all, the trip with Mark was a blast. And we promised to meet again soon. I was in a romantic mood, so I met with another regular lover, Able. He was saying, "Why don't we stop all the secrecy and just proclaim ourselves as spy leaders, who are the peacemakers and the cleverest and tell the people we won't tolerate radicalism. That would save us a lot of trouble." I told him, "Now that all the governments are essentially controlled by us, maybe its time for such a concept to be put into motion. But we would have to be careful how we did it and play down the use of MRT, which everyone is afraid of. We could simply say MRT is used only on radicals and criminals." He said, "We could still have a secret service to deal with difficult cases." I said, "Let's try it in Space first. Space is so much more manageable. And if it doesn't work, we'll go back to where we were before." I had considered such a move previously, but now was the time, just like Able said. And so, we talked over details and then loved one another again and again. After a week of loving, I told all our spies to get ready for the change.

PART EIGHT: THE COMING OUT, 2153 SPRING/ SUMMER

So, I told the spies in Space that I was assuming total control. Local leaders would remain in power but now would have to answer directly to my office, rather than make compromises with spies. It was a very tumultuous time. I proclaimed myself Empress of Space and immediately I got a lot of messages from people who wanted one thing or another. I let my assistants handle it. I told the people my vision for Space was a healthy, balanced, sane scenario.

And I told the people if they felt insane or unhealthy, rehab would cure them, and I gave shrinks power to commit problem people. But many radicals now were in hiding and very careful who they associated with. And it was more difficult to catch them. But mostly the radicals' ego caused them to reveal their true nature and they hoped to get away with it. But finally, after a few high-profile cases, most of them got the message. But some were still tough cases.

And then I assumed control of all Earth. Many of my colleague spies advised me not to proclaim myself of Emperor of all Earth and Space, but I was all in. Of course, there were many big protests, and we arrested the organizers. Finally, there was a general strike, but we arrested their organizers too and, in the end, things returned to normal. I had told the strikers they would be cut off eternal youth medicine if they didn't desist and without it, they would quickly wither and die. Many radicals who appeared at this time, claimed it was a slave society with totalitarian leadership. But I countered saying, everyone was free provided they didn't do anything radical and said I was the best leader in history. And many people thought I was a God and radicals everywhere were discredited by my even larger secret service. And most people could see that they were quite free. And I allowed opposition provided they weren't radical, but they couldn't run for office. My numerous assistants and I appointed leaders. But my machinations earned me the respect of many young thinkers who figured I was the best person for the job of Supreme Emperor. I commissioned a series of biographers who glorified my past and talked about my difficult cases as Chief Spy. I told them not to write down the radicals' names just the situation, so as not to bring the radicals into the limelight as most of them had survived rehab. But in truth, there were far fewer radicals than previously as it became obvious, they wouldn't get away with radicalism.

And I continued to work on difficult cases despite being Empress Goddess. I didn't want any challenges to my wise rule.

But I had a hard time with one radical, Dan F., who said, "All great thinking is aberrant and radical." But he didn't announce his views to anyone but my assistants. I told him, "You are on a dangerous, precarious slope." He said, "Name any great discovery in history and you would find the geniuses that discovered them, thought outside the box or were radicals in other words." I replied, "But such scientists always respected their leader who ruled them and mostly they were awarded for their contributions. As far as artists go, in the past it was mostly the same." And I said, "If you had ideas, you could OK them first with my assistants before trying to disseminate them." And I had him re-hypnotized.

And I had a problem with another radical, Suzy S. She mind read to me, "Your assistants killed my true love who just wanted to be free and to free others. I looked up the case and then mind read, "Your boyfriend wanted to run for election, proposing to replace all the spies with elected officials and he died in rehab of sheer hubris. He was really a bad ass." She mind read, "You don't care who you hurt or how many hearts you break. You are just a killer at heart." I mind read, "I brought peace to the Worlds and now because of me, everyone lives in an Utopia." She mind read, quoting Socrates, "The unthought life is not worth living." And then she ran through the window of the high rise in which we were talking and fell to her death. I have to admit her death disturbed me. But I reminded myself that I had done a lot of good for the Worlds. And sometimes one had to pay a high price for peace. And we had to move on.

Another problem was Theresa H. She supported and gave refuge to her radical lover. Her philosophy was the Worlds were boring and she wanted to shake things up. Her lover, Peter R. wrote a book about how those with good, radical ideas should have as many children and clones as possible. Theresa said, "Let's dig up the graves of famous radical thinkers of the past and clone their DNA. People like Copernicus, Galileo, Plato, Jesus and so on. Of course, they had just discovered Jesus' grave in India. And many wanted to clone him. And 20 years ago, they'd found Plato's grave" Peter said, "You and I are both rich so let's make it happen." So, at this point after listening passively, I mind read actively to Peter and Theresa and told them, "The World is at a very high quality of life, it is Utopia. We don't want radicals rocking our boat." Theresa mind read, "I think you spies are preventing radicals from succeeding and that's why you are in our head. No wonder the World is so boring." Peter mind read, "We'll start a fund for cloned geniuses and copy each one hundreds of times!" I mind read, "You are both out of control crazy. I am sending you both to rehab. Theresa mind read, "It's a pogrom on intellectuals." Peter mind read, "You spies are evil." I had caught the two of them just in time…

Then I was dealing with a radical freak, Bibi. She owned a chain of bars and had radical bands playing in her bars. A number of budding radicals came to her bars. There were many people associated with the bar that had to be sent to rehab. Bibi, the bands and many of the clientele. It was a big case for me. Bibi mind read, "But we are peaceful and clever." I mind read, "You're just a shit disturber." She said, "It's just like the book 1984 and you are Big Sister." I said, "That book is banned now. It is a book of evil and confuses the younger members of our cities."

And I thought to myself, I hope this book I'm writing doesn't fall into the wrong hands. I was surprized the radicals were so easily vanquished. But who knew what the future would bring? Some of my spies harbored radical ideas and had to be watched.

And as Supreme Emperor, I announced a new set of proclamations. Like no more thinkers, all thinkers would be sent to rehab. Those who had thoughts that differed from the official philosophy, would have to keep such ideas to themselves. We didn't need any more science. We lived in Utopia. And we didn't need new music or novels. We had more than enough. Many people didn't agree, but as I thought, they kept their thoughts to themselves.

And as Supreme Emperor I ordered all types of artists to promote me and my rule. So, they painted pictures of me and sculptures too. And writers wrote biographies of me and chronicled my most difficult cases, back when I was just a spy.

Then I was back with my lover, Able. He said, "I don't know how you get away with stopping all original thought!?" I replied, "Most absolute rulers in history did the same, my rule is nothing new, rather it is a continuation of the past only with a different level of technology. But I am thinking of rolling back some of the science in our World today. And I have brought a peaceful Utopia to the World and my reign will last for Millenia. You'll see. And I hope you continue to be part of it." Able said, "You have certainly saved the World from Armageddon, and we are all grateful to you. And there are fewrevolts, your spy system is still effective." And Able and I loved one another hard for a week.

My next problem was with a woman who had secretly organized a cadre of original thinkers, but my spies got wind of it And I mind read to her, "You are guilty of treason." She mind read, "If I can't think I don't want to live." I mind read, "Rehab will give you a new perspective and make you whole. You are lucky that I am so enlightened." She mind read, "I'll kill myself rather than go to have my mind basically destroyed." I mind read, "Why not give rehab a chance?" And so finally she agreed. And I sent her cadre of thinkers to rehab as well.

And I kept promoting free love amongst the people. I told them, "Make love and not be a thinker. And I kept taking more and more power for myself. Finally, I did away with all national and state/provincial governments. Just the Mayors and me. And the Mayors had to take an oath of loyalty to me. Of course, some Mayors acted up, but rehab solved that. I had my spies watch the Mayors carefully and most Mayors were former spies and I felt on the whole they were doing a great job. This was a huge step forward for my power. It was all a big surprise to most…

But then there was an insurrection in L.A. The Mayor, had dared to raise an army against me and had pre prepared laser weapons in secret. And he conscripted all 18 million citizens of the city. It was tough fighting him and UW forces. The fighting went street to street, apartment to apartment. His people were inspired to fight, and all their leaders told them they were fighting for free thought. And the five generals I had sent there, rebelled against me and joined the revolutionaries. So, I sent in my best troops with my friends who were generals and finally the revolt was crushed. And thousands and thousands were sent to rehab. We had to build many more mental facilities to deal with the influx of radicals. But I worried that the partial success they had would embolden others.

Anyway, my next problem was on Caliban, Moon of Uranus. Here they had declared independence. I sent my best troops, and they quickly conquered the Calibanites. And I made Caliban a rehab center. And I was reassured that future revolutionaries would be dissuaded from taking action by my conquest.

Then I was called into solve a dispute between two UW Generals, both female. They were fighting for control of Ganymede. They each accused the other of thought crimes. And when I delved into the case, I found they had both become power-crazed and basically drove each other insane. But I assumed control and replaced both Generals. It was a big public relations disaster, and I sent both Generals to rehab. But I hoped the episode would also dissuade future disasters. No General wanted to go to rehab. But there were actually a small minority of people who wanted rehab. I wanted more people to go there so I took some big successes after rehab and sent their stories to everyone to encourage people to go. I even contemplated sending everyone to rehab, but knew I'd never get away with it. Some of my assistants questioned my sanity, but I reassured them I was totally in control.

Next up was a man who claimed we all led a life of horror, and he had many people listening to his podcasts. I mind read to him, "Life is lovely!" He mind read, "Some are born to be great thinkers and you are persecuting them and killing their minds. And the worst part is you are getting away with it." I mind read, "You will have to tell your listeners that you regret what you've told them, and you are very sorry." He said, "I'll do no such thing!" So, I turned up the voices in his head until he backed down and did my bidding and then went humbly off to rehab.

I reflected people these days should know better than to try and fight the status quo. But there   always seemed to be some who were so stubborn and egotistical that they paid no heed. And about this time, I revised history classes at university to just teach the last 25 years. And especially the last four years in which I had been the #2 Spy and then Chief Spy and then Supreme Emperor. Anything before that was bunk, they were taught. And most students were advised to not study history at all and just study modern studies. And were taught not to think, but rather to memorize the knowledge that was taught to them. Knowledge was the goal, with the facts of our time. Including many cases who were sent to rehab and how they felt much better afterwards. They were taught mental health was the prime objective of all humans. And slowly but surely we were making people sane.

Then I was dealing with a woman who was a singer with many fans. But after a visit with spies, she told all her followers to do acts of civil disobedience and overthrow the regime. We acted quickly and shut down her website. But the damage had been done and I blamed the spies who had visited her and sent them to rehab along with her. It was a true debacle. And many of her followers disturbed a lot of shit and we had a hard time quelling these protestors, and shipping them off to rehab.

Next, I was faced with a man who said, "He'd built a temple in honor of me, the Supreme Empress. But he portrayed me as the "Great Destroyer." And many people came to the temple to worship me as the Goddess of Chaos and Doom. Clearly, he misunderstood me and my mission. So, I closed down the temple and sent him to rehab. And I was largely shrouded in secrecy and many people had a mistaken impression of me. I wanted them to think of me as a gift who was a Goddess who had come from deep Space to help humanity grow up. And there were more and more temples built for me that I approved of.

And the next case was a meeting with the Mayor of X-city on Luna. This mayor kept telling me to move on to a new phase, that would amaze all my followers. He mind read, "Specifically, you should spell out what the future would be like for the benefit of your admirers." I mind read to him, "We'll close down the handful of deep Space colonies. And make X-city the new capital of the Empire. A spectacular city will be built here and help us keep control of the Solar System. A fresh new start. And everyone will be required to pray at my Temples for me to bring them good luck. And there will be plenty of examples of divine intervention by me, the Goddess. And my spies will serve as acolytes in the Temples. And give guidance to the people who will all live to please me, the Goddess. The one and true divine entity." The mayor mind read, "The future sounds like it is all preordained, but brilliant." I mind read, "It will all be predictable, yes. No need of Supercomputers to do that!

Then I was meeting with the usurper of our colonies in the Centauri System by 3-D meeting tech. I told him we feared the vast distance would lead to insurrection. But we had perfected 3-D meetings years ago and now used it to drive this man crazy and get in all the heads of the people there to get them all to return to Earth. I didn't want to let a cancer like that grow. And I did the same with the other five colonized Systems. Everything was under control.

Next, I was confronted by a man, George, who many thought was a musical prodigy. I mind read to him, "We have no use for more music, we have plenty of it and modern-day society was all about blending in and joining the group and thinking as one. He was wise enough to apologize to me and his followers and admitted he'd been out of line. So, for a change I didn't have to send him to rehab like I did with nearly all budding famous musicians. I liked him so much, I appointed him to a spy position so he could catch other would-be famous musicians. But his fans were angry with him, calling him a "phony" and one day he was assassinated. The killer was quickly arrested, and she said, "George was a sell-out. And he'd broken her heart. So, she went quietly to rehab, and I did not clone George.

Then I met a musician, Amy who played instrumental music only. No vocals. She had a lot of followers, but they were calm and not fanatical, like many of the pop music followers. So, I mind read to her, "Is this then the future of music?" She mind read, "Yes, it is calm and dreamy, just like the future prognosis from you your highness." I had told the people, "Future people will be laid back and dreamy and prosperous and happy, including those who had been sent to rehab."

And people could sell their nighttime dreams, and these were mostly innocuous. But there were a few dreamers who dreamt dangerous visions. Like Randy who dreamt of true love that went beyond the love of the UW. In the dream the lovers proselytized true love, and everyone wanted to find true love. I mind read to Randy, "True love is not something that should be broadcast to the Worlds. It will make others feel inadequate and lost. It is too much pressure to love like famous couples. And anyway, people should love me, the Empress above all!" But I let him go with a warning. And had him hypnotized.

My next challenge was a woman, Jewel, who claimed she had used MRT to get men to fall in love with her. Of course, MRT was illegal except for the spies. And I mind read to her, "You've

basically, boasted of breaking the law." She mind read, "But MRT love is glorious and is so pure and refreshing and everyone is truthful and real, not phony." I mind read, "Modern love is glorious enough, to improve it with MRT would be blinding and confusing and obsessive and would be a violation of privacy. It would drive people completely crazy." She mind read, "I loved with MRT and it was pure sanity, the Worlds could benefit from this great technology. Why hide it? And radical thinkers would join the whole, which would make your job a whole lot easier. I know you want us all to live as one under your leadership." I mind read, "Of course I've considered it, but ultimately it is too crazy." And I only mind read actively with assistants and problem people. Most people we watch, we mind read passively and they don't even know we are there. Of course, I mind read with my lovers, but I didn't tell her that. But I sincerely believed MRT was to be used for the elite spies only who were well-trained and sane. And I had her hypnotized.

Next up was a nascent colony, "True City" on Titan, Moon of Saturn. They had created freak animals who they hunted with bows and arrows and ate. I mind read with their leader, Samantha, "Why kill sentient creatures and cause them pain when you can eat synthetic stem cell meat?" Samantha mind read, "Humans lived for nearly all their history as hunter-gatherers. And besides hunting is exciting and the freak animals who we hunt are dangerous and could breathe fire." I mind read, "Samantha, the human race has evolved. We don't eat real meat anymore." She mind read, "But the people here are engaged and interested in hunting. And there are hardy new plants which we can also eat." I mind read, "Let the freaks you've created be destroyed and your people eat like every other person does these days." And I sent Samantha to rehab, along with her assistants.

And then I had to deal with a woman, Charlotte who mind read, "The spies were in my head, but I ignored them and loved my true love despite their protestations." I mind read, "You have to go along with the spies, or they will drive you insane!" She mind read, "But my love is a genius scientist." I said, "We are watching him, too. He is involved with teleportation technology which we have recently banned and practitioners who had to recant and admit they were against the future of humankind. You and your boyfriend will go to rehab."

And next was a woman who said, "She wanted to help those who had come out of rehab, to help them retain who they were before." I mind read to her, "You are an anathema to the modern Worlds, and you need to go to rehab." She mind read, "What you are doing is not right and I have millions of followers who support me." I said, "You'll recant and tell your followers you were mistaken. And then you'll go to rehab."

And then I was confronted with a woman, Enigma, who insisted on "being on the dark side." She said, "Human history was dark and mysterious, but that's what people wanted." And she said, "Humans were an enigma, and the future is highly uncertain." I mind read with her, "The vast majority of humans want to be good and have no use for the dark side. The dark side is wholly unnecessary and is evil." She mind read, "But it as a mysterious World and who knows how it will end up. The future is a mystery." I mind read, "The future is no mystery and will turn out to feature me as the ultimate leader deep into the future. It is all preordained." She mind read, "I don't think you can control everything." I mind read, "Just watch me!" And I sent her to rehab.

PART NINE 2153/2154 FALL/WINTER

And then I was dealing with a man, Barry, who mind read to me, "We live in a Utopia, but we need to keep evolving as humans." I mind read, "No, "There is no reason to improve on humanity as a rule. Just keep sending those who don't follow the script to rehab to make sure everyone is on the same page. Our Utopia will last for thousands of years and I will rule for thousands of years, myself." He said, "It sounds like stagnation to me." I mind read, "The economy will continue to grow, and peace will continue. Soon everyone will be relatively prosperous." Barry mind read, "So we are giving up our freedom in exchange for wealth?!" I mind read, "People today are freer than any other point in history. Total freedom is anarchy, and we can't have that." He mind read, "In in much of recent history people were freer." I mind read, "The spies were always there with hypnosis and then neo lie detectors and disappearances and people committing suicide, dying young of cancer, or backing down, or 'selling out.'" He mind read, "But why can't you tolerate other opinions?" I mind read, "One Supreme Ruler is the only way to bring peace, for certain. And I tolerate other opinions within reason." He mind read, "Three of my friends were sent to rehab and they went in as lions and came back like kittens." I mind read, "But you were wise enough to bring up your grievances with me directly rather than just madly spouting negative thoughts. So, I'll let you go anyways. Consider this to be a warning." And I had him hypnotized.

Next up was a fighter in no holds barred fighting and he had been champion for three years. He had a lot of fans, but then his ego blinded him, and he ran for the city Mayor of Dallas, saying Dallas would pull out of the UW System and he convinced the Mayors of three other American cities to join him. I mind read with him, "If elected what would you do?" He mind read, "I didn't realize you spies got into peoples' heads if they ran for office." I mind read, "You are going to opt out of the electoral race, and I don't want to hear from you again. Stick to fighting in the ring." And I figured I'd nipped him in the bud. And hypnotized him.

Then there was a poet who seduced the most beautiful women of our time. And he said, "I am the Worlds' best lover. And many women wanted a piece of him. *Times magazine* voted him the sexiest man of our time. And he was so rich that he was able to have 25 clones and the women kept lining up for a piece of one of the clones. The clones had their memories updated with his memories and vice versa to make a kind of "Super lover." I figured he was too powerful, so I mind read with him, "You have to quit promoting yourself as the World's greatest lover and stop loving famous women." He said, "I'd rather die than cease loving my women. I of course mind read to him, "If you didn't back down, I would drive you insane." He tried to bargain with me mind reading that, "I would be satisfied with my favorite 3 women. And my clones will also pick three." I mind read, "At least its something. Yes, I will accept that." So, he couldn't say I was unreasonable, but in truth I didn't see why so many women wanted to love him. He certainly didn't turn my crank and I thought his poetry really sucked. And I had him hypnotized.

And my next case was a man who called himself Buddha, who carefully wrote a treatise, "To Those Who Would Be Free," in which he argued that if you could free your mind and not be beholden to others, it would be the best of all possible mindsets. He recommended spending time meditating and clearing one's mind and forget about materialism and forget about modern love which entailed mostly empty one-nightstands. He had a small number of associates. And had millions of fans. Many people it seemed were disillusioned with this light I had created. And I figured he was a danger to the UW. So, I mind read with him, and he mind read, "I wondered when the much-vaunted spies were going to get in my head actively. I suppose you'll tell me I have to withdraw my treatise from circulation and my life is forfeit. I mind read, "You can enjoy the pleasures of this enlightened age and live in grace and comfort, but you need to distance yourself from your treatise." And he smashed his head against the wall and broke his neck and died. I was hardened and largely unaffected by his suicide. I figured I'd done the right thing.

Next in line it was the case of a man, Phillip who said, "We are on the road to nowhere." And told people, "And our Goddess, the Supreme Empress, was a phony who just cared about her own power." And he told people, "To become suicide bombers and give the phony Empress a message. And suddenly there were hundreds of bombers." I got in his head very loudly and mind read, "You are a danger to society, but rehab will cure you." He mind read, "You are not a God." And off he went kicking and screaming to rehab. As for the bombers we arrested them all before they could set off the bombs.

And then I found myself dealing with a woman who was an evil scientist who was spreading disease around which inflamed one's brain and caused irreparable damage and death. She had poisoned the water supply with her disease. I got in her head and mind read, "Why would you do such a thing?" She replied, "I am sick of humanity and their pettiness and insolence and greed." I mind read, "You have to work with scientists to come up with an antidote. And then you will go to rehab." She mind read, "Death is glorious! And there's no way I'll help you. And I hope I have made my mark on history. She killed countless thousands." I told the people, "See what evil lurks…" And I said, "My regime has virtually wiped out evil, but it still exists." Some people said that I was behind the poisonings to justify my heavy-handedness. But I was really pleased that I had caught all evildoers before they could do much harm, with this exception. I blamed the local spies for not identifying her intents. They all said, "She suddenly snapped and went insane."

That was followed by a case involving a comedian, Anabella. She said, "Life was just a joke, and one should laugh at everything and everyone including the Supreme Empress Goddess. And it didn't matter what one did; it was all a joke. And there are no footprints in the sand… And if they were forcing you to be serious, you should just kill yourself." I confronted her and mind read, "Life is glorious, especially during my reign of peace and enlightenment." She mind read, "You are the one who made a fool out of many intellectuals and have basically banned creative thinking. So, there's nothing left to do but laugh cynically." I mind read, "We've achieved all we can through science and the arts and there's no need for further works/research. Let's just live for peace and sex and parties and fun." She mind read, "You are just a power-crazed, insolent anathematic persona." I mind read, "Well no World is perfect for everyone. It's a case of the greatest good for the greatest number." She mind read, "But most people today are insane." I mind read, "They might be crazy, but they are prosperous, and most are happy." And I figured Anabella was a threat to civilization and decided to stop her in her tracks and sent her to rehab.

My next case was 3 women who claimed to be witches. They said they could do magic. Like predict one's future and created an app which allowed one to throw fireballs and lightning strikes. And they could animate the dead. And could heal all mental problems. And so on. I mind read to them, "Are you evil?" One of them mind read to me, "Why are you asking? Are you some kind of spy?" I was dressed in normal clothes with one of my lesser-known faces, and I mind read, "Let's just say I am affiliated with the UW." Another of them mind read, "It is impossible to hide our thoughts with your MRT. But we are good witches." But I sensed, she was lying. And I mind read that same witch, "If they worshipped Satan?" The third wish mind read, "Truthfully, we do. Evil is good and good is evil." I mind read, "We don't need evil personae in these Worlds. But the first witch mind read, "But we are healers and let people free their minds from this boring culture." I mind read, "I am sending you all to rehab."

Then I was mind reading with the Mayor of San Francisco. She mind read, "That my city was now all gay including me. But many people want my job, and I am sure I will lose the next election." I mind read, "Why don't you set up a gay colony on Titan and pick the leaders from among your many allies. Perhaps many of your opponents would want to go to Mars, and so won't want to run against you." And I mind read, "You should also appoint many of your opponents to be ambassadors, to avoid having them run against you!" He mind read, "They are both good ideas. I have to try something, for sure." And the Titian colony was not the first all gay city in Space and only gays were allowed in, and they had gay children only. The future of gays looked bright.

I was then confronted with another hell-raising poet. He said, "This world needs a shake up. We need to be ruled by the best lovers, not the tyrannical Empress. It's a cold World of one-night stands and there is not enough love to go around." So, I confronted him with mind reading; "You are a sap who wants wimpy leaders, but you forget that the powers that be are serious about power and won't give it up to a bunch of wimps. And I am sending you to rehab."

My next problem was with a man who had an attitude problem. He mind read to me, "I am very clever and I want more money from the government." I mind read to him, "Why should we give you more money?" He mind read, "I want to start a colony on Luna for the imaginative people only and we would vet everyone who came there." I mind read, "This World already has too much imagination. We wouldn't want such a colony. It would be too dangerous, too many cooks, spoils the broth." He mind read, "My colony would inspire many and improve their thinking." I mind read, "People these days are inspired enough and live quality lives. No need to rock the boat. And you are going to rehab."

The next case was with a woman, Claudia, who organized protests against my Imperial self. The protestors wanted freedom of speech.

We brutally cracked down on the protests and I faced the organizer and mind read with her, "How did you ever think you would get away with it?" She mind read, "We are an advanced civilization and deserve free speech. If there are no critics, there can be no improvement." I mind read, "Modern society is approaching perfection and if there was free speech, like hate speech and destabilizing concepts, the Worlds would fall apart."

She mind read, "But you spies have created a civilization of slavish people. You turned everyone into a wimp, while you spies are yourselves free and happy." I mind read, "We spies don't allow ourselves to be completely happy and we all toe the line. And control our egos."

Then I was dealing with a woman who knew the secret of hypnosis and got a number of people hypnotized to bomb the government buildings on Io, Moon of Jupiter and then she announced she was the new Mayor of Io #4. The revolution spread to the other 5 colonies on Io, and she seized the armory and so outfitted people with lasers. It was a careless mistake leaving the armories lightly guarded. But I ordered the UW Space fleet in full force to hit them, and the UW troops made short work of the rebels. It was a lesson for me. Henceforth vetted UW troops would police every Space colony. And I revealed the whole situation on Io, to the people of Earth and Space and made it clear that revolutionaries would be executed after a MRT test showing them as guilty. Many people were afraid of me, the Supreme Empress Goddess, and few had the stomach to challenge me. And that was good.

And then I was challenged by a woman who claimed to be an idiot savant. She mind read, "I am a genius computer engineer but have no talent for the arts. Computer engineering is now banned, and scientific progress has ground to a halt, and I am useless in the modern-day scenario." I mind read, "We already have reached the peak for what humans can do in science. You need to evolve to fit in with our modern-day Utopia. Learn to have many lovers and go to many parties. And enjoy this luxury life. Buy an air car and travel around in Earth and the

Solar System and make new friends who are people just like you." She mind read, "But science is the thing that has driven all progress. Why should we suddenly abandon the quest for knowledge? It's just like the fall of the Roman Empire a new dark age and stagnation are coming." I mind read, "As I have mind read, Science has peaked, and you had better get with the program if you want to survive." And she mind read, "I'll try my best!" And I had her hypnotized.

Next up was a woman who claimed to be a talented poet, but I read her poetry and found it was poor, not very intelligent, so I didn't worry about her. But she mind read, "I am prepared to die for trying to get elected to Mayor of Tokyo. I mind read, "No one dies anymore for their beliefs. That is passe. And democracies only elect our brilliant spies to office in the Grand Empire and never in history has there been such brilliant leaders. You have to find a leader you like and follow them and the Worlds will be your oysters." She mind read, "But all the leaders seem to be the same." I mind read, "All modern-day leaders are geniuses, what's wrong with you?" She mind read, "It just doesn't seem like my kinds of Worlds, I feel like an alien." I mind read, "These Worlds have never been your kind of World. You are just a freak." She mind read, "How can it be a World in which I fit in nowhere?" I said, "You can't just expect the World to be as you wish. You are a maniac." And I dismissed her with a warning, "Don't try and disturb shit." And had her hypnotized.

And then I was up against a woman, the Mayor of Mars #9, who mind read, "I am bored by this World." I mind read, "There are many worse things than being bored. Why not try some neo stimulants which will make you feel more interested in these Worlds. And you could try and volunteer to help those who are sent to rehab try to acclimatize themselves to their new reality. You can be their angel." She mind read, "When I got to be Mayor on Mars #9, I thought I had it made, but I am just suicidal." I mind read, "You need to go to rehab to refresh your philosophy." And so that was that.

And then I had to deal with, Conn, who was a philosopher who had said, "I believe in a World that is like the High Middle Ages with noble knights and brilliant women." I mind read, "Few people today have studied history, in fact we spies are thinking of banning history altogether. But the Middle Ages was misery for almost everyone, whereas modern day people live gracefully and comfortably, and no one is destitute or has to work hard." He mind read, "I'd like to have important work to do, but it seems we are all at loose ends." I mind read, "We have liberated people from toil and hard work and created a perfect World. In actuality we are all spoiled rotten and are all greedy for pleasure and material possessions, which we have in abundance. But few complain about modern reality." He mind read, "I just wish there were alternative Worlds to go to!" I mind read, "Humanity decided 50 years ago to not have alternative Worlds, believing we are all in these Worlds together. Everyone was in the same boat. And alternative Worlds would have thinking holograms which were clever slaves who would be abused by people. So, holograms are out. And each colony and city, has their own style for the people. You should travel more and get with the program." And I dismissed him. And I reflected we were not tortured with many philosophers. In general people were content to involve themselves in their local milieu. And if they strayed from goodness, they'd go to rehab. And I had him hypnotized.

ADDENDUM

And my last big action was to forbid all my spies from using MRT on me. Not active, nor passive. This upset a lot of my spies. But I told them I must have total power… Not even my clones could mind read with me, henceforth. But I could still mind read with them, passively.

And I was building temples everywhere for worshippers to worship me and I had my millions of children staff the temples. My kids were nearly all born a year or less ago and could prove themselves to me. And my clones assumed the leadership of many important Mayoralties. The majority of my 210 clones were produced in just the last year with all my memories. But I had to watch my children and clones carefully lest they try and overthrow me. Basically, they watched one another closely. And a couple of clones had to be executed for plotting against me.

Meanwhile my subordinates were sending numerous people to rehab, but we'd passed the peak and now had less cases than before. New science was dead and so too the arts. One of my subordinates suggested, "We force problem people to admit they were certifiably insane. Like paranoid schizophrenics and have them take heavy tranquilizers." I said, "Why don't we just continue as we are with rehab!"

And I could write several books about the cases my subordinates solved. And finally, I stopped actively spying and concentrated on governing, building my Grand Utopia. And basically, we had wiped out radicals. No new radicals were being born; we had designer babies and the "babies" when born were all good-looking and had mainstream thoughts. I'd purified the human race. And I looked forward to centuries of peace and prosperity.

In hindsight, the future couldn't have been different. A Supreme

Goddess Empress was inevitable. A woman who was peaceful with a maximum EQ and IQ. I could imagine many Dystopias and many of my cases described in this book imagined Dystopias, but it was destiny to build an Utopia like the one I had created.

As the centuries passed, very little changed. People got richer, everyone got richer. And I ruled on, and there were fewer and fewer radicals and ruling was a cinch...

www.ingramcontent.com/pod-product-compliance
Lightning Source LLC
Chambersburg PA
CBHW051851130726
47987CB00002B/785